# Reflections of Winnsboro

by

Bill Jones

with

Maryann Miller

# Published by MCM Enterprises
# Copyright © 2017 by Bill Jones

All rights reserved. Without limiting the rights under copyright reserved above, no part of this publication may be reproduced, stored in or introduced into a retrieval system, or transmitted in any form or by any means (electronic, mechanical, photocopying, recording, or otherwise), without the prior written permission of both the copyright owner and the above publisher of this book.

ISBN-13: 978-0986426919 (MCM Enterprises)

ISBN-10: 0986426911

Edited by Audrey :Lintner at ALTO Editing
Formatted by Art Nelson & Maryann Miller
Cover design by Dany Russell
Cover photograph by Maryann Miller

# ACKNOWLEDGMENTS

Bill Jones would like to thank all the people who have shared stories and pictures with him throughout the years, with special thanks to ***The Winnsboro News***, where his weekly column, "Historical Reflections," has been published since 1985. Some of the pictures included in this book were borrowed, with permission, from the newspaper archives, while others are from Bill's private collection.

The Winnsboro Center for the Arts graciously provided a meeting place for Bill and Maryann to work on this book, and they both are deeply grateful for that support.

As a member of the Winnsboro Preservation League and the Winnsboro Heritage Society, Bill Jones would like to thank members of both organizations for their support through the years as he documented and preserved the history of Winnsboro.

# DEDICATION

## To Betty Jones

# Index

Introduction by Maryann Miller

Chapter One – In the Beginning

Chapter Two – Early Communities

Chapter Three – The Coming of the Railroad

Chapter Four – The Bowery on Market Street

Chapter Five – Notable People in Winnsboro

Chapter Six – Other Wood County Notables

Chapter Seven – Schools and Places of Education

Chapter Eight – Prominent Men and Businesses

Chapter Nine – Outlaws and Other Criminals

Chapter Ten – Special Places and Events

Chapter Eleven – Agriculture; A Way of Life

Chapter Twelve – The War Years

Chapter Thirteen – The Oil Boom

Chapter Fourteen – Sports and Sports Stars

Chapter Fifteen – Things of Note from the 1900s

Chapter Sixteen – Famous People from Winnsboro

Chapter Seventeen – The Building of the Arts District

# INTRODUCTION

History is not just a lot of dates and facts crammed into books. History is about people and the situations in which they found themselves; things that made a significant mark on a specific time. It is also about what we can learn from knowing the people, as well as the events that impacted and shaped their lives.

That is what Winnsboro Historian Bill Jones has spent most of his life doing, writing the unique history of the town from his own experiences, as well as those passed to him by long-time residents.

It was an honor to work with Bill on the *Images of America: Winnsboro* book that was released in 2013, and, at the time, we thought that at some point we needed to expand on the stories that he told to illustrate historic facts. Bill Jones is an extraordinary storyteller. There isn't a time where you can meet Bill for a "hello" on the street, or sit down to have a cup of coffee with him, that he doesn't have a few tales to share about the people and the situations and the incidents that made Winnsboro what it is today.

That is what you will find in this book; stories of the people Bill has known in his life, as well as about the people who first settled in Winnsboro. You can walk around Winnsboro and the surrounding area and read the more than thirty-five historical markers that Bill has placed, but they are just a hint of the full story. Here in this book, you can find out more about the Indians who first lived in this beautiful part of the country, the two men who paused to rest at a crossroads and decided to stay, the woman who convinced the railroad to come to Winnsboro, and the visits and exploits of the infamous Bonnie & Clyde.

Over the many years that Bill wrote columns for local publication, he did meticulous research, interviewed family members of early settlers, and wrote about the famous and the not-so-famous.

This book is a collection of some of those columns and stories, compiled and edited by me. Everything in the book is in his words, with only minor editing, with the exception of the last two sections of the final chapter, The Building of the Arts District. I wrote the sections on the Winnsboro Center For the Arts and The Bowery Stage because Bill had not written a newspaper column focusing on the history of either one. The only history he has written was about the building that houses the Winnsboro Center for the Arts, but because the art center is the cornerstone of the Cultural Arts District, it was important to have it included in this book.

Bill says that Winnsboro has always been home to him, so I invite you to open the book and "come home" with Bill Jones. Grab a cup of coffee and enjoy his stories.

Maryann Miller

## Chapter One – In the Beginning

The town of Winnsboro sits in the heart of the beautiful piney woods of East Texas, just ninety miles east of Dallas and one hundred miles west of Shreveport, Louisiana.

In the beginning of the sixteenth century, all of East Texas was a giant forest inhabited by mostly friendly Caddo Indians. Spring-fed streams were abundant with fish, and deer, wild turkeys, and bear roamed the countryside.

European explorers made successful expeditions through the area in the seventeenth and eighteenth centuries, and both France and Spain considered this part of East Texas "their sphere of influence." In 1821, Mexico gained its independence from Spain and made land available for colonization. However, until 1836, when Texas won its independence, migration from what was then the United States was not significant.

It was then that Anglo travelers began using creek crossings where Little Cypress and Big Cypress come together at a spot that today is six miles north of Winnsboro near Highway 37. Back in 1836, it was an area covered by swamp land and century-old cypress trees. Eventually, some people stayed in the area, and the Associated Cypress Baptist Church was founded in 1851. In those early years, it was common for folks to form a church soon after settling in an area. In addition to being places of worship, churches were meeting places for the people in the community, as well as often serving as a schoolhouse until a separate school could be built.

In the summer of 1854, William Rile McMillan and John Elliott Winn left Bellevue near Henderson, Texas in search of a new location for their business. They traveled north to Gilmer, then followed the Jefferson Road northwest toward Greenville.

Late one afternoon, the adventuresome pair reached a crossroads—the road to the north pointed to Clarksville and the Jonesboro Crossing on the Red River, the south trail led to the water port on the Sabine River, three miles south of present day Hawkins. The well-traveled path to the west pointed to Reilley Springs and Greenville. The east route extended to the port city of Jefferson, second only to Galveston as the state's most important water port.

McMillan and Winn made camp for the night on a rolling slope covered by huge oak trees near the crossroads, and the next morning they decided to inspect the countryside. They discovered that the soil was excellent for agriculture, game was plentiful, and there was a good supply of water in the area.

The nearest settlement, Cornersville, was two miles to the west. In 1861, Rev. E.H. Green of Green Hill, a community northwest of Mount Pleasant, established one of the early Presbyterian churches at Webster, three miles south of Winnsboro. In 1871, members of that congregation joined hands with the Presbyterians of Winnsboro and built a small white sanctuary at 400 Church Street. in Winnsboro. McMillan and Winn were impressed with business prospects at the crossroads, today the intersection of North Main and Pine Streets. They were successful in acquiring 361 acres of land from the William Logan estate with the crossroads being near the center of the tract.

They named the settlement Crossroads and built the first structure in the community, a mercantile business. The building was 20' x 40' with a porch across the entire front. A sign above the porch read "Cheap Cash Store." This store is believed to be Wood County's first business. Across the road, to the southwest of the store, was an excellent water well frequently used by travelers and passing teamsters who were transporting goods to the West. Dr. Joseph McGee and Andrew Vannoy operated the first sawmill and constructed a commissary store at the southwest corner of the crossroads. The first residence, a two-room cabin, was built at the northeast corner of the crossroads by McMillan, and then John Winn constructed a one-room bungalow about three hundred feet west of the McMillan dwelling.

Soon the settlement required a new name, as Texas already had a community called Crossroads. The first name to be chosen was Winnsborough in honor of McMillan's stepfather Capt. John Elliott Winn. With the new name, the post office opened March 6, 1855.

In 1859, James and Nancy Cook arrived in the new town of Winnsborough. They purchased the eastern two hundred acres of the McMillan/Winn tract, including the two-room McMillan residence, and proceeded to expand the structure to a two-story building, sporting a mixture of early Texas and Victorian architecture.

The detached kitchen was called Cook Tavern, and it was there that travelers and locals enjoyed delicious food at a large kitchen table. Cook Tavern was the only place in the frontier town to acquire news via the passengers from the Jefferson to McKinney stagecoach. A two-horse stage coach carrying up to four passengers, would stop at the tavern and patrons would relate news from the East. Even though the establishment was called a tavern, it served no alcohol. Nancy Cook was a teetotaler, but she named her place a tavern, as that was customary back then.

## An early settler

Rufus F. Stokes, who was born in 1823, settled in this area before the arrival of McMillan and Winn. Stokes acquired land and appeared to be a learned person. He became a justice of the peace in 1868 and was involved in early Winnsboro civic activities. His great-great grandson, the late Billy Ben Smith, shared some family history with me.

Rufus and his wife, Susan, had a large family that included two sons, Bill and Ben. Bill Stokes was involved in just about everything that went on in Winnsboro, from schools to city affairs. He also once served as a Wood County Deputy Sheriff.

Before 1920, W. H. "Bill" Stokes owned Winnsboro's largest barbershop. It was located in the rear of the building at the northwest corner of East Broadway and Market Streets. The Star Barbershop, which was luxurious for a town as small as Winnsboro, had five barbers. Upon entering the shop, customers would take a token with a number on its face. A large clock in the rear was numbered one through forty and was used to notify waiting customers when their time arrived to receive a shave or haircut. When each barber finished with a customer, he would push a button, and the clock hand would spin to the next available barber.

There were five large bathtubs in the rear of the barbershop, and on Saturdays men would come in for a shave and haircut and bath. The shop also had a place where clothes were brushed, pressed, and sprayed to alleviate any odor from the fabric. At that time in history, many customers only took a tub bath on Saturdays, so this may have been a Saturday ritual for many of them.

The barbershop had an elaborate electric and plumbing system, which was unusual for the 1920s. Stokes had a boiler in the back that provided steam for pressing clothes and hot water for bathing. By this time, the city did have sewage facilities that took care of the wastewater.

Early barbershops—or tonsorial parlors as they were sometimes jokingly called—did more than offer a shave and haircut. They often served as an unlicensed doctor's office, offering treatment for boils, ringworm, infections, and bloodletting. Few barbers had any medical training, but offered relief to customers at a cheap price. By the 1950s, medical practice by barbers had just about disappeared. State and federal laws prohibited barbers from practicing home-remedy medicine.

Once more homes had their own indoor plumbing and bathrooms, men stopped coming to town on Saturdays for a shave and haircut and a bath. The local barbershop was no longer a favorite place for gathering.

## First the area belonged to the Indians

Long before any white settlers came, the Winnsboro area of East Texas was inhabited by Native Americans. A community of Caddo Indians known as Nandacao settled at the site where Winnsboro was later founded. An Indian trail passed through the site, originating from the east and heading to the headwaters of the Sabine River near what is now Greenville, Texas. This trail was known as the Caddo trace.

The Native Americans were here from around 700 A.D. until the 1850s. They raised families, played games, taught their children the Caddo way of life, conducted religious ceremonies, grew old, and buried their loved ones on sacred burial grounds for over 1,100 years. The Indians were primarily farmers and had two major tribes. The Kadohadacho lived in large villages along the Red River near the present-day Oklahoma/Arkansas border. The other tribe was the Tejas, or Hasinai, Caddo who lived farther southeast.

Those Caddo Indians of East Texas formed the Hasinai Confederacy, which extended north to the Red River, west to the Trinity River, south to near the headwaters of the Naches and Angelina Rivers, and east to what is now Shreveport, Louisiana. The

Caddo Indians developed a superior form of government, traded with the Plains Indians and made a network of trails to all sections of their confederacy. Texas was admitted to the union in 1845, and when that was ratified in February, 1846, the federal government forced the relocation of both tribes of the Caddo Indians onto the Brazos Reservation. In 1859, many of the Caddo were relocated to Oklahoma and were concentrated on a reservation located between the Washita and Canadian rivers.

All that is left of the Caddo Indian influence in the area are some artifacts found along the creek and what is now City Park. The Winnsboro Preservation League erected a historical marker to acknowledge the legacy that the Indians left.

The significant historic periods that affected the East Texas Indian civilization are:

- prior to 1803 when the Louisiana territory belonged to France;
- the influence of Spain until the Mexican Revolution of 1821;
- Republic of Mexico from 1821 to 1836; the Republic of Texas from 1836 to 1845; and
- the period that followed after Texas joined the union as the 28th state.

Under America's fifteen-million-dollar land purchase, the Louisiana territory west of the Mississippi River included all tributaries whose water flowed into the Mississippi from the West. Thus, what is now Winnsboro became part of the Louisiana territory because Cypress Creek, north of town, flows into the Red River and then into the Mississippi.

However, Spain also claimed much of this land, so the area between Louisiana and Texas was known as "no man's land." It would take until 1841, during the days of the Republic of Texas, before the boundary would be legally aligned with the United States.

By the early 1800s, the once-powerful Caddo Indians were thinned by war and pestilence. Their homes, land, and wealth had been taken by European Americans. About 1819, the Cherokees, pushed from their homeland farther east, moved into an area of East Texas between Nacogdoches and Tyler, joined by the Kickapoos and Delawares.

The few remaining Caddo survivors roamed the forest like wild animals, hiding from the white man's vengeance.

In 1839, problems arose with the Cherokee Indians. They had been promised a parcel of land between Nacogdoches and the Sabine River to the north, but the treaty was never ratified by The Republic of Texas. Since the Cherokee were losing the land promised to them, they became hostile. President Lamar ordered a force of about five hundred soldiers to subdue the Indians, and many Cherokees were killed.

The remaining Cherokee Indians were told they could either leave Texas or be killed. Many of them chose to relocate and followed a defined trail north to Oklahoma, which is remembered as one of several "Cherokee Trails of Tears." Many of the sick and old died on the trek; according to legend, a Cherokee rose, the state flower of Georgia, grew in every spot a tear fell on the Trail of Tears. Today the flowers grow along many of the trails that the Native Americans took west, and some can be seen on fences along county roads east of Winnsboro.

## Jefferson – Gateway to Texas

Before Jefferson was established, Caddo Lake was created, a byproduct of a log jam that extended up the Red River for over ninety miles. Called the Great Raft, the log jam diverted water from the river's main channel into the Caddo chain of lakes. This enabled flat-bottomed steamboats to travel to the lake seven to eight months of the year, depending on rainfall and the level of the lake.

Heading west from Shreveport Louisiana, the boats used different routes to enter Caddo Lake. One route was by way of Cross Bayou and Cross Lake; then to the Soda Lake Chain and into Caddo. Another route went up the twelve-mile Bayou, through Soda Lake, and then into Caddo Lake. At the entrance to Caddo Lake, steamboats had to pick their way across a shallow stretch called Albany Flat.

Steamboat captains came to Caddo Lake in the 1830s, bringing economic development to the area. Until the mid-1840s, Caddo Lake ports were regarded as the head of waterway navigation. The first ports of call on the lake were Potter's Point on the north and Wray's Bluff on the south. After Texas' independence, and the migration of Americans that followed, ports of call included Port Caddo, Smithland, and Swanson's Landing.

In 1845, a steamboat reached the East Texas town of Jefferson, located thirty miles from Caddo Lake on

Big Cypress Bayou, with 130 passengers. More boats followed, and along with them came prosperity and hope for those who decided to stay in East Texas. Cotton became an important commodity and was shipped by boat to New Orleans and other destinations. This was the beginning of the boom in Jefferson, Texas. The city flourished and soon became a major port.

By 1849, steamboats were arriving on a regular basis, and Jefferson became the head of navigation for Caddo Lake.

Jefferson also became important as a land center for commerce. A series of trails that could be used by wagons led from Jefferson through Clarksville, Paris, Gilmer, Webster, and Winnsboro, and then on to the line of Army forts west of McKinney, Sherman, and Dallas-Fort Worth. At this time, Jefferson was comprised of sixty houses, stores, warehouses, a gristmill, and a sawmill. The boat trip between Jefferson and New Orleans has been described as five days of uncomfortable travel.

Jefferson became a wealthy city during the 1850s to the 1860s, and was the largest trading center in Northeast Texas, second only to Galveston as a shipping point. Cotton, hides, wheat, processed meat, and other items came to Jefferson as a distribution point. Goods would be sent first to New Orleans, then put on ocean-going ships to be sent to all parts of the world.

On the return trips from New Orleans, over the difficult lake channels, manufactured goods arrived in Jefferson to be distributed to the outlying settlements to the west. The western line of Army forts were supplied needed military equipment and other items. Large steamboats often waited for days in Jefferson to be unloaded, then reloaded with raw materials. Meanwhile, wagon trade became so heavy that roads leading to and from Jefferson endured traffic jams that extended for miles west of the port city.

The Western frontier hamlet of Jefferson began to resemble New Orleans with its Greek revival homes, New Orleans-style restaurants, saloons, quaint shops, theaters, social life, and lighted streets at night. During this period, Jefferson entertained a notable variety of well-known people. These included steamboat company presidents, U.S. presidents Grant and Hayes, English author Oscar Wilde, and industrialists John Jacob Astor and W.H. Vanderbilt, among others.

During the Civil War, Winnsboro and all of East Texas played an important role in providing raw materials for the Confederate soldiers through the port of Jefferson. Markets for East Texas cotton were found in Great Britain and France. By 1864, Northeast Texas and Northwest Louisiana were supply lines for Southern troops through Jefferson and Shreveport. The Union desperately needed cotton from the South for the clothing mills of New England; instead the cotton was destined for the Confederacy. President Lincoln reacted, ordering an assault by the Union Army and Navy on Northwest Louisiana that later spread into Texas. The attack was made by 36,000 Union soldiers under the command of General Banks, supported by a fifty-six-ship flotilla under Admiral Porter.

It was an attack that was destined to fail. Confederate troops sank a large steamer in a narrow strait between Shreveport and Natchitoches, Louisiana. The stalled Union naval vessels were ordered to turn around to protect ground forces. General Banks led his troops into Northwest Louisiana and East Texas. A major battle occurred near Mansfield and Pleasant Hill Louisiana, resulting in a humiliating defeat of the invading army by a smaller Confederate force; that brief East Texas excursion was the only one of the war to occur here. However, water travel through Alexandria, Louisiana was now blocked. The only method of getting war materials to the Southern forces was by overland transportation.

After the Civil War ended in 1865, Jefferson once again became a busy port for exporting raw materials and a port of entry for manufactured products. By then, Jefferson had a population of ten thousand, and thousands of immigrants in search of new land and homes passed through the city to venture deeper into Texas.

In 1872, the Great Log Raft on the Red River was fully cleared and the lakes on the Texas side gradually began to drain back into the Red River. The water level in the lakes fell by only a few feet, but steamboats could no longer travel the Big Cypress Bayou to Jefferson. Only the dead hulls of beached steamboats remained, resting on the shallow lake bottom.

## Chapter Two - Early Communities

Those who traveled to East Texas in 1854 rode down rough dirt roads, camped or slept in log cabins that usually had dirt floors, and visited with people they met along the way. Most were newcomers to this vast domain called Texas. Anglos, mostly southern immigrants, came here for the rich fertile land and to expand slavery. Money was scarce. Maybe a few people had a little gold, but barter was the common form of exchange. Everyone packed a revolver or rifle in this wild country. People had plenty of land, but they were poor. They drank coffee made from parched corn, ate a lot of cornbread, since wheat was not grown here, and, if fortunate, they had a cow to provide milk and butter. Fruit, except for what grew wild—berries, plums, and grapes—was virtually unheard of.

I remember a story told to me by the late M. D. Carlock as related to him by his father. The senior Carlock said he joined his stepfather, Major Pitts, the founder of Pittsburg, in a caravan of four to five wagons that were carrying salt to Fort Richardson at Jacksboro. After encountering daily problems with Indians, they returned with sacks of wheat to be ground at Major Pitts' gristmill at Leesburg. He had noted that wheat flour was a scarce and costly item in early East Texas, and saw the opportunity to take advantage of that need.

Travel through Texas followed trails that were first made by Indians. To my knowledge, the only well-

## Reflections of Winnsboro

defined road was the old San Antonio Road from Nacogdoches to San Antonio. In the late 1830s, five or six trails left the port of Jefferson and spread out in several directions to the west. By the time of the Civil War, some paths became pretty good roads, with bridges across streams.

Structures in this area consisted of a one-room log cabin where all family members slept, and they survived on cornbread, meat, and sweet potatoes. The settlers who traveled to this area usually followed a wagon on foot. They would pile their scant belongings in the wagon that was pulled by oxen. If they brought a sow, or a litter of pigs, the pigs rode in the wagon and other livestock followed the wagon. After walking several hundred miles to reach this new place, the settlers were exhausted; many of them suffered from fever and malnutrition. The poor slaves who accompanied them were ragged, hungry, and spiritless.

After a few months of trying to survive in this rugged environment, some families gave up and returned to their original homes. Those who stayed built lean-tos and crude cabins for protection from the often-harsh weather. The log cabin was cold in the winter and hot in the summer. Most of them had a fireplace at one end of the building that was used for warmth, cooking, and usually provided the only light. Open windows were covered by wooden shutters or animal skins and much later replaced with glass.

It's hard to know what possessed these early pioneers to take on the arduous journey to Texas. Did they come just for the cheap land?

Farmers who did stay would plant their first crop of corn by burning out a cane break, and when the fire was out, there was a clean field covered by ashes that was as loose as plowed ground. The farmer would then take a sharp stick, make a hole in the ground, drop a grain of corn into each hole, then cover the holes with dirt by using his foot. Under the spring sun the corn shoots would grow an inch a day. The planter had neither plow nor hoe at first, and he would knock the surrounding weeds down until the corn became large enough to shade the other growth.

When the roasting ears began to appear on the corn stalks, bear, deer, and coons would begin eating the crop if it was unattended. To prevent this, the farmer would tie an old hound dog in the middle of the patch of corn. The dog would bark and howl all night and scare the animal intruders away. The family would then eat fresh corn, roasting the ears in ashes inside the cabin. Even before the corn was hard, they were making cornbread. Once the farmer survived their first year, often they could start acquiring farming implements from Jefferson.

Some of the early communities that formed around East Texas after the Texas Revolution were Webster, Perryville, Peach, Merrimac, and Shady Grove.

Ruben Elledge was a transplant to Shady Grove from Georgia. He personified the image of a successful farmer who had an intense interest in advancing the betterment of his community. In 1850 he donated land and build a one-room log structure to be used for educational and religious purposes. It had split pine logs with auger holes in the rounded side of the log with a pin inserted in the holes as legs for the benches.

The Elledge school, thought to be the first institution for learning in Wood County, was headed by a schoolmaster named William Webb who lived in the school church building. It has been said that Prof. Webb often received his tuition fees in the form of corn, potatoes, or other agricultural products.

In August 1850, Ruben Elledge, joined by Henry Stout, D. O. Norton, Peter Gunstream, Jonathan Russell of Webster, and probably J. P. Cain, met with about twenty other men a few miles northeast of the present Mineola for the county's first election. Elledge served as the chief justice of Wood County from 1851 to1860.

In addition to donating land for the school, Elledge donated adjacent land for the Shady Grove Cemetery. This well-maintained burial ground is one of the oldest cemeteries in Wood County and is still being actively used.

Shady Grove's Methodist congregation organized a church at the Elledge schoolhouse in the 1850s, then in the 1860s the W. M. Ashby and L. W. Wiley families gave 1½ acres of land across the road to the north of the school to build a Methodist Episcopal Church. Vault Cassell contributed one acre of land on the west side of the church grounds in 1915 to be used for church purposes. In 1952, a new sanctuary was erected at the same location, but religious services are no longer held at the Shady Grove Methodist Church. The church building belongs to the cemetery Association and serves as a meeting place several times each year.

Perryville was established at the location of a sawmill that was surrounded by a large tract of virgin pine timber that was one hundred to one hundred fifty years old. A man named Parry is said to have operated a steam-powered sawmill there and employed a number of hands to work in the mill. People began referring to the area as Parryville. In 1853—a year before the founding of Crossroads—a road was built by slave labor from Gilmer to the community that was later renamed Perryville. The road also branched west, going to Quitman, Webster, and Winnsboro. The road enabled farmers to ship cotton and other produce to a market at Jefferson.

### Early Perryville settlers

A man by the name of W. C. Corbett traveled by ox wagon to the settlement in 1853 from his Mississippi home. Another man, John Lawrence, built a sawmill on a spring branch east of Perryville in 1856. W. E. Webb, brother-in-law of Lawrence, established a mercantile store, which is said to be the first store in Perryville. Other pioneer families in Perryville were named Hester, Byron, Bailey, Spence, Richards, Price, Schrum, and Morrison.

By 1906 the prime grade timber had been cut and sawmill operators moved to a different area where the virgin timber still flourished. At one time, there were five small gins in Perryville, and by 1900 the community had two churches, a school, and a large store operated by J. P. Byron. Perryville's population at that time was one hundred.

**Reflections of Winnsboro**

John Bailey, one of Perryville's first settlers, moved from Georgia to Wood County in the fall of 1851 and settled one mile west of Perryville on Katie Creek. Just before reaching the new homesite, his family stopped take part in their first religious service in East Texas near the old Jefferson Road, using logs for benches. Bailey purchased 346 acres of land for $1.75 per acre, and it took him six years to pay for that land. For the first four years, the entire Bailey family lived in a sixteen-foot log cabin.

Early settlers also established other churches near Perryville. In November 1879, thirty-eight Perryville-area Methodists gathered for an organizational meeting of the Marvin Chapel Episcopal Church of the Methodist Episcopal Church South. From 1879 to 1887, church meetings were conducted at brush arbors, in homes, or at the school. Later, members of the congregation built a church building with rough timber that was fifty feet long and thirty feet wide. J. D. Hollinquest donated the land, and a number of church members offered financial support and labor to build that first church.

In 1871, philanthropist Nancy Cook gave one acre of land at the Northwest corner of West Elm and Church streets to members of the Methodist Episcopal Church. By 1880, membership had grown and sufficient funds were available to construct a one-story, 40' x 60' sanctuary. It was a white wooden structure that faced West Elm Street. That building met the spiritual needs of Winnsboro Methodists until 1904, when a new and larger building was constructed at the same location.

**Bill Jones**

## The East Point Community

The community of East Point was an early Wood County settlement where truck farming was the major business. If you went outside in the spring when the area was first settled around 1844, you could have picked up the scent of new-plowed ground and seen the farmer with his big straw hat following the mule up one row and down another from daylight to dark.

Squatters lived in the Merrimack Perryville area in the late 1830s after the Texas Revolution. Henry Stout, who came to East Point in 1844 or 1845, is recognized as the first permanent settler. He received a large section of land for service as a scout for Gen. Sam Houston during the revolution.

According to existing records, the town's name was derived from its location on the east point of an early settlement. By the mid-1850s a number of settlers had established homes around what is today called East Point. Henry Stout's water-operated gristmill is said to have done a brisk business. Sawmills and gins began to appear a little later.

Before long the town started to change as log cabins were replaced with nice homes and well-kept farms began to dot the countryside. Roads were improved and a few bridges spanned the creeks.

Now it was time for the community to build a school and a house of worship.

The first school in this area was established at nearby Shady Grove in 1850. It was a tuition-based school that lasted four or five months out of the year. Education in East Point had its beginning on

December 30, 1878, when the I. F. Taylor family gave land to be used for educational and religious purposes.

In 1884, the Texas legislature ordered counties to be divided into school districts. The East Point School District Number 36 covered 5,136 acres. Masonic Lodge members offered their two-story lodge building adjoining the church for educational and religious purposes. The first school building was a two-room frame structure, and as enrollment increased, it was replaced by a four-room school.

By the late 1940s, the community's population began to decrease in enrollment, and the school became smaller. School trustees decided they could no longer afford quality education for their children and agreed to consolidate with Winnsboro ISD. On December 17, 1953, all claims to school land ownership was conveyed to the deacons of the East Point Missionary Baptist Church for the sum of fifteen dollars by the Winnsboro ISD. The school building was moved to Winnsboro where it served as the high school homemaking cottage for many years. Today, the wellhead in front of the church is the last visible sign of the school.

On Saturday, September 24, 1893, the Missionary Baptist Church of Christ at Little Hope met in conference and, by request, extended an arm of the church to the Baptists of the East Point community for the purpose of receiving members. Twelve East Point charter members were received the following Wednesday by Little Hope. Then on Sunday, October 1, 1893, baptism was administered to the charter members at the Stinson Mill Pond, which is located one mile east of the present Little Hope Store. Letters of admission were granted by Little Hope Baptist Church, and the new members named their church East Point Baptist Church and agreed to meet once a month.

The first meetinghouse was a 30' x 31' white wooden frame building with double front doors. Benches were constructed from fourteen-inch rough lumber. A simple pulpit, benches, and a large wood stove were the only interior furnishings.

In 1928, after thirty-five years of service to Christianity, the first church building was replaced by a new structure. Then in 1952, the present church building was completed and extensive remodeling and additions have been made since then.

Today, East Point Baptist Church has an active enrollment of 145, and after 102 years the church continues to offer spiritual guidance to the community. The people still hold on to the cultural values of their ancestors, and East Point is a proud community that has two churches. It is the home of Capt. Henry Stout State Park and has a number of small stores. They don't have log rollings and barn raisings anymore, but do have good neighbors who are always ready to extend a helping hand.

## Immigrants made Texas great

We native born and raised Texans are a rare breed. We are proud of our heritage, although over 97% of our ancestors were living elsewhere when Texas declared its independence from Mexico in 1835; as well as in 1836 when the heroic battle of the Alamo was fought and Texas' independence was won at the battle of San Jacinto.

In 1835, the population of infant Texas, destined to become a Republic and later an American state, was less than thirty thousand in the entire Mexican province encompassing what is now Texas. By 1847, after Texas was annexed to the United States as the twenty-eighth state, the population had increased to one hundred forty thousand and the diverse population was comprised mostly of Americans and Europeans who had immigrated to Texas.

The nearest settlements to present-day Winnsboro during the period of Mexican influence that are seldom mentioned by historians, were in an area in Northeast Texas known as Pecan Point, White Rock, and the Jonesboro Crossing on the Red River. At one time, the entire land area was claimed by both Arkansas and the Republic of Mexico. The land that was claimed by Arkansas included a part of Eastern Oklahoma, and in Texas the counties now known as Bowie, Lamar, Red River, Cass, and Camp. At the time, Mexico lacked the manpower and means to challenge its territorial claim this far north of San Antonio de Bexar. After 1825 Texas became a part of the state of Coahuila with the capital at Saltillo, five hundred miles from San Felipe.

## Hopewell Cemetery

Cemeteries are among the most valuable of historical resources. The names on the tombstones serve as a directory of early inhabitants of the area.

Tombstone designs and cemetery decorations tell a story of a different culture that helped shape the history of Texas. Many of the nineteenth-century family cemeteries established in and around Winnsboro by early pioneer settlers have simply disappeared and now occupy space as a meadow, pasture, or wooded area.

Some time ago I had an enjoyable afternoon visiting the Hopewell church and cemetery, which is located eight miles west of Winnsboro on County Road 4870. The road in front of the church is part of the original roadbed that once extended from Jefferson to Greenville and all points west. Through the years, this historic artery, which dates to the early 1840s, has been called either the Jefferson, Greenville, Dallas, Webster, or Pleasant Grove Road.

While slowly walking through the well-kept Hopewell burial ground, I passed the graves of soldiers from the Civil War to Vietnam, county and state officials, clergy, teachers, farmers, children taken by illness, and those associated with violence and tragedy. They are all here, the pioneer men, women, and children who blazed a trail to this new country, cleared a field, built a house and raised their families on this good earth. The later ones, who established schools and raised their children and grandchildren, sleep in silent slumber at this hallowed place of rest.

There are many residents of the Hopewell Cemetery who made contributions to their community during their time in life, but one that stands out in my mind is George Turner Hinson, a Wood County patriot and an outstanding Texan. There has never been anyone who loved his country more than Mr. Hinson.

## Reflections of Winnsboro

A descendent of early county pioneers, George Hinson was born northeast of Pleasant Grove. He served as a teacher, farmer, railroad engineer, and is known as one of East Texas' great boasters. Hinson was elected to the Texas Legislature in 1951. The Speaker of the House appointed the well-respected gentleman from Wood County to several important committees, and at the time of his death in 1970, Representative Hinson served as vice chairman of the Higher Education Committee. Better teacher salaries and advancement in Texas education are the two things I most remember about Mr. Hinson. After visiting the cemetery, I wandered over to the grove of trees behind the church and stood in silence for a moment, thinking of how life has changed since the outlaws Bonnie and Clyde hid out in the patch of woods on a number of occasions while evading the law during the early 1930s.

According to existing records and stories that have been passed down, the Hopewell church of the Primitive Baptist faith first met on May 1855, in a grove of oak trees near where the present church building stands. In the fall of 1855, a one-room log house was constructed which served the congregation's needs for years. In 1876, John Moore donated three acres of land adjoining the church to be used for the church and cemetery purposes; the first known burial was that of Henry Nixon in 1879.

The log building was replaced by a much larger wooden structure and that building was then replaced in 1947. Today the church and cemetery continue to serve the community as they have for more than a century.

## Webster settlement

Three miles southwest of Winnsboro is a community that was known for well over one hundred fifty years as Webster. On one cool October day in 2010, I drove up the driveway to the residence of the unofficial mayor of Webster, and Sue Craddick Hamm stepped out to greet me. "Bill," she said, "I am so glad that the railroad in 1878 was built through Winnsboro and not Webster. I can sit on my front porch and listen to the chirping of the birds, watch the squirrels dart from one limb to another, enjoy the serenity of country living and the aroma of fresh-baled hay. If the railroad's course had passed through Webster, I would have missed all of that beauty."

Webster is recognized as the oldest settlement in the area. Settlers began arriving after Texas became a Republic in 1836. Riverboats maneuvered the Cypress Bayou and around 1837 or 1838 came as far as present-day Jefferson. When Jefferson became a riverport town, it started to flourish, and by the end of the Civil War the population had reached what is reported to be about twenty-five thousand. One of the trails out of Jefferson led further west through the village that later became Webster.

Scant information about the community has survived from the early days when Webster was a Republic of Texas settlement. The Bureau of Business Research work titled *An Economic Survey* states that Webster was settled in 1845, less than ten years after Texas won its independence from Mexico.

The road to the north from Webster, that passed through Winnsboro, led to Clarksville then northwest of the Jonesboro Crossing on the Red River. The road west from Webster led to present-day Emory, Greenville, McKinney, Jacksboro, and the fast-growing village of Dallas.

According to records that Sue Hamm has, Webster was first named Prospect Hill. She told me, "It is understandable why the immigrants selected the name Prospect Hill as there is a small rise in the contour of the land at the crossroads. It is enough to indicate a hill, and perhaps the settlers also felt there were good prospects in this new country."

When the first colonists arrived, there were still a few Indians living in the area, but they were friendly Caddo Indians. The land was rich and the game plentiful. The first newcomers were primarily from the old South where cotton and corn grew in abundance, and they carried on that farming tradition in this new area in East Texas they called home.

### Prominent People Around Webster

Uncle Henry Robinson, who founded the community of Pleasant Grove and built the first house in Winnsboro for W. R. McMillan in 1854, owned a blacksmith shop in Webster. Robinson arrived in the area around 1850. Capt. Jonathan Russell came to Wood County in 1848 and settled at Webster. He fought in the Mexican war, commanded Company B of the Texas Volunteers during the Civil War, and served as a member of the

Texas Legislature before and after the war. Capt. Russell participated in Wood County's first election in 1850.

In 1855, a post office was established at Prospect Hill, with Thomas Sadler as the first postmaster. The following year, the name of the community was changed to Webster, named for the American Statesman and orator Daniel Webster who had died in 1852.

Gilbert and Mary Ann Clements Matthews, late of Georgia and Alabama, came to Jamestown in Rusk County in 1851. The town was located midway between Tyler and Henderson. In 1854 the family moved to Prospect Hill and purchased a large tract of land, and Gilbert was instrumental in developing the village into a trade center, renaming the settlement Webster. Matthews built a fashionable home and a large commissary store that also served as the post office. His son-in-law, Robert King Bradshaw, ran the store, and Gilbert became the postmaster. Records do not indicate ownership, but Gilbert influenced a cotton gin and a blacksmith shop. Farmers came from miles around to the gin to have repairs made and to trade at the Matthews & Bradshaw Store. Gilbert helped to promote the idea of the school and a Methodist Church. All the while, he was developing a successful cotton plantation.

In 1858, Hinton and Elisabeth Craddock arrived in Webster from Sampson County, North Carolina by way of Henry County, Alabama, where they had spent twenty years. Hinton bought 294 acres and built a two-story house. Later he bought the Gilbert Matthew's house and another 147 acres. This was the beginning of the Craddock clan at Webster. Wortham Craddock, who researched historical accounts from the eyes of those who were there, told his younger brother, Joe Bailey, that Webster's business district consisted of a four-acre tract located at the crossroads. The town had a triangle public square, a large well and water trough in the middle of the square, and a school located in the northeast corner at the point where the Jefferson Road arrived from the east. Schoolchildren would watch with interest as immigrants, wagon trains, and military equipment arrived on a journey to the West.

Judge Will Suiter, a noted and respected local historian, taught school in Webster in 1891. He reported that the community's population of 600 to 800 exceeded the population of Dallas from 1854 to 1856. However, this is a debatable fact as Webster was never incorporated, and a population census was never submitted to the state for record purposes. Still, there is no doubt that a thriving community did exist at Webster from the 1840s to the 1850s.

The basis for Mr. Suitor's statement may have been based on the number of people who received their mail at Webster. That post office handled mail service for present day Mount Zion, Sharon, Stout, Shady Grove, Hopewell, Pleasant Grove, Clover Hill, Cartwright, and Eagle. Some Winnsboro residents also called for their mail at Webster.

In the 1850s, a typical Webster scene would include a freight wagon pulled by six to ten yoke of oxen hauling bales of cotton over the nearly impassable road to Jefferson. The driver would walk beside the animals, sometimes popping a long bullwhip above their backs, but never touching their hides with the whip. An old bull whacker once told me that if you ever struck the ox with the whip, it destroyed the animal's spirit and it was no longer good for work. At night, the oxen were allowed to graze in the open range, and the lead animal always wore a bell around its neck to help the driver locate the animals at daylight. By then, they would have recovered from the prior days' journey, which is one reason oxen were favored over horses and mules. They could pull a heavier load and recover more quickly than the other animals.

However, the ox was a slow animal, usually averaging only six to eight miles a day pulling a heavy load. Few bridges spanned the waterways between Webster and Jefferson, and sometimes it took two weeks to make the trip to that port town, especially after a big rain.

Webster was a peaceful and prosperous community nestled in the hills of East Texas and covered by tall longleaf yellow pines. But Webster would experience a rude awakening in 1861, when the winds of war descended over the village. Able-bodied men put aside their wagons and plows, fetched their muskets, said goodbye to friends and loved ones, and marched off to war in defense of the Confederacy. Most of the local folks had migrated to these parts from the old South and felt a strong allegiance to the South, although some of those who served did not believe in secession. Once the young men had left the village of Webster, all that remained to hold things together where women, children, and the older men.

A number of military units were formed in Wood County. The 10th Texas Calvary, 12th Brigade consisted of nine companies comprised of 503 men. The 1st Company, under the command of Capt. William D. McKnight of Webster, was known as the "Rough and Readies." The 7th Company, commanded by Capt. John Denton Sr. of Webster, was known as the "Sons of Liberty." Capt. Denton lived at Clover Hill but received his mail at Webster.

Men from Webster and Winnsboro trained at Camp Flourney, located east of the Quitman town site. According to records, the men of Wood County made a good showing for the Confederacy. It has been said that when the citizen-soldiers marched down the Belzora Road to board ships at Belzora Landing, they were in high spirits and shouted, "We will be home in six months."

They did not realize the bloody Civil War would last four years, and that many in their ranks would never see home again.

Reliable folklore accounts indicate that a Confederate shoe factory was located near the Tanyard Springs at Winnsboro. Animal hides were preserved through a curing method at the Springs, then made into shoes for Confederate soldiers. The shoes were transported to Jefferson and from there to a distribution center near Richmond, Virginia.

## A place of refuge

Despite the scarcity of food and medicine in this area, East Texas became a place of refuge for Confederate soldiers who were recuperating from battle wounds and avoiding capture by Union troops. War never came to Webster or Winnsboro, so it was left unspoiled by actual combat. Fierce battles took place in southern Arkansas and south of Shreveport near Mansfield, but this area of East Texas never suffered from the direct devastation of war.

By the spring of 1865, law and order began to suffer. Vigilance committees were formed to keep watch and prevent crime and looting; however, they sometimes became over-zealous. Such citizen groups often turned into mobs. Unionists who opposed secession, and those who attempted to avoid the struggle entirely, were harassed. Records indicate some were hanged for their beliefs. Webster appointed a trusted local citizen to handle law enforcement, but he had little authority over mob rule. Everyone tried to arm themselves against roaming gangs.

During the Civil War, the communities of Webster and Winnsboro suffered many shortages. Coffee became a luxury and substitutes such as okra, parched acorns, or parched sweet potatoes were used. Baking soda became an impossible luxury. Calico at Matthews and Bradshaw store was priced at fifty dollars a yard in Confederate currency. People wore homespun clothing as they had done in colonial days. Shortage of medical supplies had people relying on their own medicine made from roots and herbs.

By April 1865, the Civil War struggle came to an end when Gen. Robert E. Lee and his soldiers laid down their arms at Appomattox Courthouse in Virginia. The surviving "Boys in Gray" began the long walk home, most without food and many sick and without proper clothing. Most of them walked home barefoot.

# Reflections of Winnsboro

## After the war

After the Civil War ended in 1865, Texas, along with the other states of the former Confederacy, suffered through five devastating years of Reconstruction, ending in 1870. Rules imposed by the victorious Union forces were intolerable, and those who lived in the conquered southern states either obeyed those orders or citizens would find themselves before a firing squad or hanged. Martial law had been imposed, and everything that had belonged to the Confederacy became property of the United States government. Confederate currency could no longer be used as legal tender, and all Confederate laws were declared invalid. Rebel soldiers were denied the right to vote, which caused a deep resentment across Texas and the rest of the South.

For the first four to five months of reconstruction, a total breakdown of law and order was the rule. All officials throughout the South had been elected under Confederate laws, and therefore the legality of these officeholders had been invalidated. Some Confederates were not ready for reconstruction and opposed what they called "Yankee Rule." They refused to follow instructions or appear for work details. Gangs roamed the countryside, robbing people, killing some, and inflicting inhumane treatment on the freed slaves. Things became so bad in this part of East Texas in 1865 to 1866, that the commandant of the district of Texas, Col. George C. Custer stepped in. Custer, who later acquired the rank of general and was killed by Indians at the Little Big Horn, issued orders that either the rebels obey rules of order or they would face the consequences of their actions.

Wood, Titus, and Hopkins Counties were hot spots of Southern sentiment during Reconstruction. Texas governor E. J. Davis, an unpopular carpetbagger appointee, sent a letter to Bodark Carter of Wood County that stated, "You are infernal rebels and don't deserve protection of the government. If I had my way, I would hang every last one of you."

After Reconstruction ended and the U.S. Army troops left Austin, the unpopular Davis remained governor through 1873, with help from the militia. When his term ended, he hightailed it out of town on the first stage.

## New businesses

Somewhere in 1868 or 1869 the Matthews and Bradshaw enterprise came to an end at Webster, and the new business moguls were two Jewish merchants named Goldman and Ferguson. They owned two large wholesale warehouses and transported goods from Jefferson and the Belzora Landing to Webster for storage. Later, the items were distributed to Dallas, McKinney, and points to the west.

R. C. "Tubby" Smith, my high school history teacher, whose family were some of the first Wood County settlers, told the following story. He said a large livery stable was located south of the Webster Square near the crossroads with pens of horses, mules, and oxen. Smith said the animals were of a good bloodstock, probably some of them owned by Goldman and Ferguson for their freight business. Horse traders hung around the stables, always looking to make a trade.

After the Civil War, Winnsboro nearly died. The town was one of Wood County's hotbeds for secession sentiment, and many local young men had been casualties of the war. Some people left because of the constant demands of Reconstruction authorities. Things became so bad with population loss that the Winnsboro post office closed in 1868 and then reopened again in 1874. For nearly seven years, most Winnsboro residents received their mail at Webster. On the day the Union Army moved out, the people of Webster and Winnsboro celebrated like it was the Fourth of July. Leaving with the soldiers were the carpetbaggers and others from the North who had been installed as officeholders during Reconstruction.

By 1870, most area waterways had bridges, ferries, or shallow water crossings. Investors developed a stagecoach line from Jefferson to Mount Pleasant, and another that passed through Gilmer, Webster, Emory, and Greenville. Stagecoaches had seating for six people, with a bench on top for the driver. Coaches passed through Webster daily heading to the East or to the West. Way stations, to provide fresh animals, were established at intervals along the routes because horses and mules could not maintain a rapid pace much longer than ten to fifteen miles.

Blacks were the people who suffered the most after Reconstruction. Abraham Lincoln's

Emancipation Proclamation in 1863 ordered them to be freed from slavery. Then, in 1865, the Fourteenth Amendment prohibited slavery in the United States. But it wouldn't be until after the Civil War ended that freedom became a reality for American Blacks.

The problem subsequently became that the Blacks were free without a place to go. Most had no money, food, shelter, or jobs, and few could read or write. Folklore accounts tell of freed slaves camping in the forest, surviving only on what nature provided. Where could they go and how were they to make a living since the federal government failed to provide for the needs of these now free people? Some former slave owners offered the freed men employment as sharecroppers, and other freed slaves were allowed to buy small parcels of land and make payments to pay it off. However, most of them took any available job at starvation wages.

In about 1880, Sie and Sarah Jones acquired land and created trustees to form the Colored Methodist Episcopal Church of America. According to limited information that has been passed down by longtime members of this church, it was thought to be first organized in 1883. Services were held in a private home under the direction of Rev. C. F. Moore. The services were only conducted once or twice a month, but it was a beginning, and Rev. Moore led the small congregation for a number of years. Some of the known charter members were Angelina Wright, Carolyn Darden, Sie Jones, and Fed Smith.

It is not known when, but the name of the church was changed to Hynson Chapel CME church, honoring Rev. S. J. Hynson, who was pastor of the church and a driving force during the time of the construction of the sanctuary in 1896.

During those early years, folks would come to the house of God from miles around on foot, horseback, or wagon. It was a time for prayer and fellowship and the ladies would tell each other about what they were cooking or canning or quilting or what they were making for the winter. The men talked about crops and farming or about possible jobs.

Today Hynson Chapel CME Church continues to serve the spiritual needs of the community just as it has since 1883.

As business began to expand, Webster agriculture and livestock became even more important to this area of East Texas. Cleared land around Webster and Winnsboro was white with fields of cotton, while other fields were filled with corn, peanuts, and tobacco. The bottomland had crops of sorghum, sugar, and ribbon cane. Almost everyone had a milk cow, hogs, and several head of livestock, but the cattle industry had not developed because of the difficulty of getting stock to market.

Webster continued to be a thriving community until the decision was made to have the railroad go through Winnsboro instead of Webster. By 1881 most Webster merchants closed their businesses or moved to Winnsboro. Goldman and Ferguson was located on Main Street in Winnsboro until 1890, when they sold their stock and moved to Dallas. There they became business tycoons. At that time, there was nothing left to hold the crossroads community of Webster together, and soon the post office closed. It was about this time when someone said, "There is nothing at Webster but Craddocks and catalpa trees."

Webster was the site of the first public school in Wood County. A two-acre location at the northeast corner of the town square was set aside for a free public school. Other communities had schools, but they were subscription or pay schools. Webster had a Black school located southwest of the town site near the Mount Zion church and several Black residents of Winnsboro can trace their lineage to that community.

The Webster Cemetery is located about three hundred yards east of the town site on the south side of the abandoned Jefferson Road. It is on a sloping hill dotted with oak trees. Many of the markers have been gone for years, and all that remain are scattered rocks with depressions where graves have sunk over time. The only visible grave is that of Mary Ann North Clements Matthews, daughter of David Clements, the brother of Sam Clements—whose son was known as Mark Twain. She was buried next to Amelia and Mary, both slaves who were friends. All died of fever in 1857 over a span of three weeks.

When I wrote the stories of Webster for the Winnsboro News, I dedicated to them to the memory of my friend, Joe Bailey Craddock, who knew every creek, hollow, and family history of anyone and everyone who ever came this way. He loved this land called Webster.

## Early churches

In 1872, Presbyterians from Webster and Winnsboro met in a conference presided over by E. H. Green of Green Hill. The Webster congregation and the assemblage from Winnsboro agreed to join hands and build a house of public worship. Land for the church was a gift from philanthropist Nancy Cook. The small sanctuary constructed at 400 Church Street. was a white frame building two stories high and 40' x 25'. The lower floor was comprised of two rooms with a staircase going to the upper floor, which was probably designed to serve as living quarters for the pastor. The upper floor supported a spiraling bell tower that extended twenty feet above the roofline, sticking out in the midst of two-hundred-year-old oak trees.

Through the years, this little temple, the first house of worship in Winnsboro, also served as a community center as well as a spiritual center. Methodists who organized in 1857 met there, and Baptists, organized in 1859, also held religious services in the building for worship. Both the Methodists and Baptists went on to build their own sanctuaries in 1880. Early Christian church followers used the premises for their services and eventually organized the Central Christian church at this location 1893. They then built their present sanctuary in 1894.

Bells ringing from the belfry announced all occasions—funerals, weddings, fires, religious and public meetings. The church often served as a school prior to 1880. It was a busy place in early

Winnsboro. The church still stands at the corner of West Pine Street and Sage and continues to be a busy place, offering services as well as out-reach to the poor and a thrift shop.

In 1907, when most of the businesses had moved from up on the hill further south to be near the railroad depot, the Presbyterians acquired three lots at the southwest corner of Chestnut and Myrtle Streets for a new building. They then sold the Presbyterian lot—including all improvements near the city cemetery—to John Templeton for $400.

Henry Mitchell contacted Templeton and agreed to buy the church building for $250. Mitchell moved the structure, rolled on sweetgum logs drawn by horses, to 2404 West Pine Street. The building, with an added addition, served as the residence of the Henry Mitchell family until 1958.

## Chapter Three - The Coming of the Railroad

The railroad officially came to Winnsboro in 1878 but it was forty years earlier when the Texas Railroad, Navigation, & Banking Company was chartered to build railroads in Texas. This was ten years after the first public railroad was chartered in the United States. Despite the charter from the Republic of Texas, the Texas Railroad, Navigation, & Banking Company collapsed without ever building a railroad.

On September 7, 1853, the Buffalo Bayou, Brazos, & Colorado Railroad Company began to operate between Harrisburg, which is now Houston, and Stafford's Point. The first locomotive, named the Sherman, made the initial twenty-nine-mile trip. This was the first railroad to operate in Texas and the second to operate west of the Mississippi. It is also the oldest component of the present Southern Pacific Railroad Company.

By the end of 1861, there were nine railroad companies with 470 miles of track laid in Texas. Most of the rail activities seem to be around Houston, where population and commerce was the greatest. A general land-grant law passed in 1852 authorized sixteen sections of land per mile for any railroad company chartered to build a railroad in Texas; a section of land constitutes 640 acres. By 1882, between twenty-seven million and thirty-seven million acres of land had been granted to railroad companies, who received about $1.34 per acre when they disposed of the land.

In 1876, Nancy Cook of Winnsboro heard talk of a railroad being built west from Jefferson. She went to officials of the East Line and Red River Railroad and made an offer to give them right-of-way if they brought the railroad to Winnsboro instead of Webster. She would do this if they would allow her to determine where the depot would be built. Another part of the deal was an offer of half interest in one hundred acres to be developed as a town.

Nancy Cook's offer was accepted and the railroad came to Winnsboro.

The East Line & Red River Railroad was to go from Jefferson to McKinney. A work gang of one hundred fifty laborers began removing timber, performing grading work, and building bridges across waterways in preparation for laying track. In the area around where the men were working tent cities popped up. One large tent served as a dining hall, another as a hospital, and other tents were living quarters for the work crews. As the tracks were laid, the tent cities moved to a new location to lay more track. These work camps had a man who served as a peace officer, sometimes referred to as the Railroad Bull, and it was his job to prevent violence.

A short distance away from the other tents was one that was often filled with loud noise and fiddle playing at night. Those who desired a glass, or a bottle, of whiskey could get it there. Card games and other games of chance awaited those with a gaming spirit. When construction of the railroad lines moved, this "den of fleece artists" would move with the camp, but they never pitched their tent too close to the others.

The late M. D. Carlock once related a story that his father had told him. His father had worked as a laborer, building the East Line from Pittsburg to Winnsboro. The elder Mr. Carlock related that half of the crew were natives of Ireland who came to this country in search of better economic conditions. These Irishmen were a good-natured, strong, and healthy group of men who worked ten to twelve hours a day. They had no family ties in this country, so they lived in tents and ate their meals in the company mess hall. Many of those workers died in a smallpox epidemic, and each morning a burial group would remove bodies from the hospital and bury them in the railroad right-of-way which became their final resting place. A self-appointed chaplain would say words over the bodies and offer a prayer. The dead were then covered by earthmoving equipment. With a trace of sadness in his voice and eyes, Mr. Carlock said to me, "Loved ones in Ireland never knew what happened to them."

After two years of hardships laying rails across swamps in bad weather and ill health, the men brought the East Line to Winnsboro in the summer of 1878. The little town's uncertain future was now assured with the coming of the railroad.

As soon as the depot was built and the trains started rolling in, all the businesses on North Main and Pine Streets relocated, quickly building little wooden shanties near the railroad tracks. Winnsboro soon became a major shipping center, and farmers would bring their products to the new depot to be shipped west. Once the trains were running regularly, there might be a time when at least twenty-five carloads of lumber would leave Winnsboro every day to go west for building needs in Dallas. The largest lumber mill in the state of Texas was Ragley Lumber Mill, owned by Wolfgang Ragley, who came to Texas from Pennsylvania after fighting in the Union Army. Later he moved to Dallas, where the Ragley family became very prominent residents.

While still doing business in Winnsboro, Ragley had a railroad tram that brought lumber from his mill to town. In 1896 he sold the tram to Schlueter and Whiteman, who then sold it to the Texas Southern Railroad company in 1902. At that time, the tram carried peaches from the community of Peach, which was the largest peach-producing center in Texas. Later, the Texas Southern became the Marshall & East Texas railroad. It traveled from Winnsboro to Marshall and operated until 1917.

Every morning, except Sunday, a passenger train would leave Marshall at 8:00 a.m., headed for Winnsboro. The train consisted of a combination baggage and mail car, passenger car, and a coach. It had a seating capacity of seventy. There were twenty-four stops between Marshall and Winnsboro, and the train always stopped in Winnsboro because it had a reputation up and down the line for fine food. On October 15, 1915, the Marshall and East Texas Railroad suffered a disastrous train wreck in which several people were killed and a number injured. Damage settlements and court costs were over $250,000, which put the railroad into receivership. In later years, the trains did not run on schedule, due to a number of problems, including bridges that were burned down, making it impossible for the trains to pass. Locals started referring to the M&ET as the Misery and Eternal Torment Railroad.

The Ragley Mill had a log engine that was known as the Ethel Ann. The engine brought huge logs by rail from lumber camps at Merrimack, Jim Hogg, and Peach to the mill in East Winnsboro from 1890 to 1902. The narrow-gauge steam engine was powerful but slow, powered by a piston drive for each wheel. Locals referred to the engine as the "Shay." It was common on a Sunday afternoon for ladies to stroll around town in their church finery and they would sometimes go to the depot to see the Shay.

With so many farmers coming to town to ship their goods on the railroad, there was an increased need for blacksmith shops to take care of broken wheels and axles as wagons would sometimes break down under the load. The street that is now Franklin Street from Broadway to Elm Street at one time had as many as five blacksmith shops. That section of the street became known as Smoky Row because of all the smoke that was generated by the fires that the blacksmiths used.

The original John Johnson blacksmith shop was one of the five that operated on Franklin Street. This was from 1899 to 1914. This blacksmith shop became one of the biggest businesses in town, employing eighteen men, who did blacksmithing, wood work, building plow stocks, and repairing wagons and buggies. By 1911 the blacksmith shop expanded into one of the biggest in the United States, later serving as the town's first auto garage.

## Uncle Jim & Aunt Lulu Moore

Jim and Lula Moore, better known by area residents as Uncle Jim and Aunt Lula, were a part of the Winnsboro scene for sixty years. Jim, son of Elbert S. Moore, was born in Winnsboro on September 7, 1863. Jim attended a subscription school at the southwest corner South Broadway which is now Carnegie and Chestnut Streets. Classes were conducted in a two-story gray frame Masonic Lodge building. The bottom floor was used for school purposes, religious meetings, city affairs, and as an opera house. An opera house provided a sense of urbanity and many small communities used them as an enticement for the railroad companies to establish a stop in their villages. Traveling troupes of performers would come on the trains, put on a show or two, and then move on.

As a young man, Jim helped break ground where the First National Bank of Winnsboro stands today to create Cook Field, which was surrounded by an iron fence. Later, Jim assisted his father in a successful saddle business, Moore Saddle, which had a reputation throughout East Texas of producing a superior saddle.

In November 1886, Jim married Lula Martin, who would become Winnsboro's beloved Aunt Lula. She was born July 27, 1867 in Alabama and moved to Dallas in 1869. She spent her childhood in nearby Ellis County.

Lula and Jim operated the Commercial Hotel, which was located west of the Carnegie Library. Both buildings were razed in 1967 to make way for a grocery store. Drummers, arriving by rail, made it a point to stop in Winnsboro and spend time at the hotel with the friendly hotel proprietors. The rooms were clean, the service excellent, and the famous Moore dining room was known for its great food. The dining room seated one hundred guests, and often patrons were waiting in a line to be seated.

Uncle Jim operated a dray line for twenty-five years. He met the two passenger trains daily, delivered ice, hauled light freight, and offered a taxi service. In 1921, Lula and Jim tired of the hustle and bustle of hotel life and retired to their two-story home at 115 Sage Street., which later became Winnsboro's most popular room and board establishment. Aunt Lula continued to serve outstanding food every day, and Uncle Jim's old drummer cronies stayed with the Moores while calling on area merchants.

After months of retirement, Uncle Jim became bored, and the city appointed him Winnsboro's first traffic officer, a post he held until his death. Many pedestrians and motorists heard the shrill blast of his whistle calling violators to task from his time-honored folding chair perched on Gibson's corner at the northwest corner of Main and Elm. Jim assumed the name "Cap" during the years he served as traffic officer. Cap would often scold a red-faced jaywalker, while people watched, and speeding motorists, who were gunning it through town, received stern lectures from this elderly man.

Through the years, Aunt Lula continued to operate her famous kitchen, serving daily meals to the public, but she also found time to be involved in other projects. She charted the growth of Winnsboro while compiling its history into a book. Jim and Lula were interested in education and helped promote the town's first school building, known as the TCI, in 1888, and in 1904 helped with the school building on East Pine. Even though they never had children of their own, they helped several local children, who did not have financial means, in their efforts to attend school.

Aunt Lula had the distinction of attending the first graduation exercise in 1903, and she attended each graduation after that until her death in 1947.

The couple stayed involved in Winnsboro civic, church, and social activities for as long as they could until they started experiencing a slow down their active lifestyle. Jim Moore died July 20, 1943 at his home on Sage Street, which was only three houses from the place where he was born in 1863. He had the distinction of being the oldest man born in Wood County to have spent his entire life here. Lula continue to reside at her beloved home for several more years, and then she died peacefully while sitting in her rocking chair in September 1947. She was laid to rest next to her husband of fifty-seven years in the family plot at the City Cemetery with a large assemblage of friends present.

### The Railroad Depot

**This story about the railroad depot was first published in The Centerfold - the October November December 1994 issue.**

# Reflections of Winnsboro

The railroad depot, a symbol of this community, has stood at the same location for 116 years.

In the late 1800s, the East Line & Red River Railway was reorganized and the name changed to the Sherman, Shreveport & Southern Railroad, but about 1892, it went into receivership. W. M. Giles took over the railroad, reworked the roadbed, and in 1895 made it a standard gauge operation. Later, the Missouri-Kansas & Texas Railroad bought it as a part of the Katy system. Then in 1909, they sold their holdings to the Louisiana, Arkansas &Texas Railway. The name was changed to Louisiana & Arkansas or L&A. Today, the railroad is operated by Kansas City Southern Railway Company.

Through the early years, the depot at the train station was a popular place for local boys to gather, but after passenger service was discontinued in the early 1930s, the depot was no longer the busy place it once was. By the 1950s, the great iron horse that had brought civilization and prosperity to America began to lose its place in our society. Airplanes and buses handled most of the passenger business and trucks hauled much of the freight.

Few freight trains stopped in Winnsboro, with only an occasional one stopping to deliver heavy equipment or feed, or to pick up lumber products. Small-town depots were about a thing of the past, and in the 1960s hundreds of them closed across America. The Winnsboro railroad depot was no exception, and it closed its doors. The grand old building that had once been the town's center of activity became a gathering place for vandals and hobos. The roof leaked, windows were broken, and rubbish littered the floor, making the depot an eyesore for the community. At that time, the railroad considered demolishing the building, but, thanks to the Winnsboro Heritage Society, the landmark again breathes new life. The structure has been restored by this organization, and it is the home of several quaint little shops and soon will house a museum where records of the town past can be preserved. **(End of The Centerfold Article)**

Today, the Depot houses the offices of the Winnsboro Area Chamber of Commerce, as well as the Autumn Trails Association offices. The community room is often used for town meetings, and the Winnsboro Center for the Arts conducts some of the art and music classes there.

## Winnsboro's Post Office

Before talking about Winnsboro's post office, I want to give you a little history about the postal system in the United States. On July 26, 1775, the second Continental Congress established a United States postal system that helped in binding the new nation together. Benjamin Franklin was appointed the first Postmaster General. The Postal Service continues as the second oldest agency of the United States of America.

Eighty years later, a village located on the front tier of Texas petition the postal system for a charter to establish a post office. On March 6, 1855, permission was granted to begin operation at Crossroads. The community changed its name to Winnsborough the following year. Mail came from the East by boat via the Mississippi River to the port city of Jefferson, then a stage coach delivered the mail to points west including Winnsboro.

By 1857, several businesses had opened at the crossroads and a two-story Masonic Lodge AF&M number 146 was erected on the south side of the road with the first floor serving as a subscription school, post office, and a house of worship. The second floor housed a Lodge Hall, community room, and a residence for the postmaster. Local citizens referred to the Lodge building as the "meeting house."

The postmaster had boxes for incoming and outgoing mail. There were no mailboxes at residences like there are today. Everything went to general delivery and postal patrons inquired for mail by giving their name.

During the Civil War, mail became difficult to send or receive at Winnsboro. Postage rates increased; blockades, invading armies from the North, and a scarcity of postage stamps severely hampered postal operations across the Southern states. Sometimes it would be a month before incoming mail reached Winnsboro from Virginia. By November 15, 1865, after the devastating conflict had ended, full mail service was restored across the South.

During the Civil War and shortly afterward, our little town nearly disappeared. There were no markets for most farm products or timber and things became so slow that the post office closed in 1868. Locals traveled to Webster or Cornersville for mail.

In 1874, things began to improve. New settlers arrived from the devastated Southern states in hopes of finding affordable farmland and a chance to start over. During Reconstruction, the growth was slow as most newcomers were concerned with survival, but with the arrival of the railroad markets opened for timber and farm products in Dallas and Fort Worth. When the railroad arrived, the post office moved from its prior location to a small shanty near the depot. Then in 1896, after completion of the Andrews building at Main and Broadway, the post office was located there until 1920.

The next post office address was the Robertson building at North Main, which is now the location of the First National Bank parking lot. By the late 1930s, the post office had outgrown the space in the Robertson building due to the volume of business, and once again the post office moved. It was located at 312 North Street.

Then again in 1943, the postal facilities were inadequate to handle the population increase that came with the discovery of oil in the area. The small post office struggled to handle the mail for a number of years, until about 1948 to 1949, when funds were appropriated for another post office.

In 1976, the present building was completed at 201 Locust Street. The town's official name was formally changed from Winnsborough to Winnsboro in 1893. Rural mail delivery began in 1905. Before that time, postal patrons living in the country received mail by general delivery and had to pick it up at the post office. After 1905, service vastly improved for rural mail delivery, the only problem being an adequate rural road system. After a heavy rain country roads were impassable, and many streams lacked bridges. The only way mail could be delivered to the rural areas in bad weather was by horseback, and it wasn't until after World War II that roads in the county were paved and all waterways were spanned by bridges.

## Chapter Four – The Bowery on Market Street

A few years before the saloons opened on what was called the Bowery on Market Street, two shanty beer joints opened north of town on the Mount Vernon Road at the bottom of Stoker Hill. Another road crossed at that location extending east-west and that road went to Warwick Hill which is now where West Pine Street intersects with State Highway 11. The road east pointed to Harrison Hill and went on to Mount Pleasant. Locals began referring to this area north of town as The Flats, Peckerwood Flats, or Happy Hollow.

Furman Boles once told me that two saloons were located at The Flats and another at Warwick Hill. He said that one of the Peckerwood Flats saloons was known as Paradise, and the other was called Old Glory. The sporting crowd enjoyed spending time at the Happy Hollow watering holes, and there were good reasons why the watchful eyes of the law often frequented The Flats. In addition to serving drinks, facilities for gambling were provided, and shady characters often visited the premises. All of this sparked fights and gunplay. The wagering crowd often promoted horse races from Peckerwood Flats to the saloon at Warwick Hill. Six to eight riders with fast horses would enter the race, and this soon became a popular weekend sport, with large crowds and hefty sums of money bet on who would win the race.

# Reflections of Winnsboro

When saloons first opened in Franklin County, saloon owners would provide free transportation to their establishments. Horse-drawn hacks with three to four rows of seats would come to downtown Winnsboro as far as the railroad depot and gather those who were interested in a ride to one of the social clubs. I have been told that the hacks were always full and occupants enjoyed the ride. As the Paradise driver passed through town he would call out, "All aboard for Paradise." And the Old Glory driver left town yelling, "All aboard to Old Glory."

As time went by, serious problems began to develop at The Flats. Shootings, knifings, and fights became common occurrences. It was dangerous to ride through the area, especially at night, without being armed. Finally, the citizens of Franklin County said 'enough is enough' and called for a precinct election on the wet versus dry issue.

When those two drinking areas were closed down, there was no alcohol available in or near Winnsboro until about 1890, when the city voted to allow alcohol again and that is when open saloons were once again legal in Winnsboro.

From about 1893 to 1910, folks who wandered down Market Street, which was then referred to as the Bowery, were usually armed with a pistol, especially after dark. One of the local residents said there were saloons on every corner with their cohorts of evil influence that included mysterious characters, drinking, and shooting. The better-known watering holes were the Massel, Harris, McElroy, Wright, Corley, and Milam saloons.

The Massel saloon was well-known up and down the tracks from Jefferson to Greenville as an excellent watering hole for the thirsty traveler. The saloon had a long bar which had been imported from New Orleans, a large mirror on the wall behind the bar and a stuffed alligator on a pedestal above the mirror. There were several tables and chairs for the patrons. In the back was a gaming room, with a roulette wheel and a number of tables used for poker and dominoes.

It was here that local rowdy Bud Taylor got into a heated argument with two brothers known as the Pyne Boys over a gambling debt. Taylor pulled a pistol from underneath his coat, marched them to the wall and fatally shot both brothers. Then Taylor fled town. A posse formed and followed the fugitive in hot pursuit until Taylor crossed the Sulphur River north of Mount Vernon. One of the posse members stated, "We would have caught the scoundrel, but he was riding a long-legged Kentucky stretch horse that could outdistance our smaller ponies."

It has been related by M. D. Carlock Jr. that Mr. Pine, father of the two brothers, carried a pistol in his back trouser pocket for many years, just waiting for Taylor's return so he could even the score for his boys.

If you stepped back in time and walked into one of the saloons you would hear the chatter from our customers, especially if it was a Saturday afternoon when the happy-go-lucky Irish sawmill workers came to town after receiving their wages. The gaming tables were full of those interested in a little poker action or other games of chance. Busy bartenders would provide shots of red eye, and beer at room temperature, and homemade varieties of drink. Bartenders were usually easy-going, but enforced strict rules of behavior with a double-barreled shotgun and a club that resembled a baseball bat.

There was always the strong odor of cigar smoke and stale beer in the saloons. Spittoons were placed at the bait bar rail and near each table. Around the spittoons were spots of chewing tobacco juice where bar customers had missed the bucket.

At the bar, you could buy a good five-cent cigar, order a sandwich, obtain poker chips, shoot dice, and order a drink. Seems that everyone had a chaw of Red Bull tobacco.

During the height of the Saloon Era, it has been recorded that Winnsboro saloons were highly competitive. The Harris Saloon often offered free food with regular-priced drinks on certain days, while the Massel might offer free cigars, and McElroy invited customers to a happy hour where drinks were half-price.

During that time, there were twenty or more lumber camps operating around Winnsboro, employing several hundred men. Many were transients from all parts of the United States, as well as foreign countries. The Schlueter Whiteman lumber mill was busy in the years when heart pine was plentiful. At one time, this mill was one of the largest in the United States and employed a majority of the lumbermen in the area. They came to town on Saturday afternoon looking for a good time, mostly to drink and gamble, and may have visited every saloon in town.

Cotton farmers also came to town, and Main Street in Winnsboro in 1900 was a busy place on market days – Mondays, Wednesdays and Fridays - when wagons of cotton would be brought to town along the dirt streets. There were a number of cotton gins in and around Winnsboro where the cotton would be processed. While in town, some of the farmers would also visit the saloons.

The city marshal, John Cain, did not bother the revelers as long as they stayed on Market Street and did not bother the citizens on Main Street. Those that did venture where the refined citizens went were put in jail, and the jail was often filled by 10:00 p.m. on a Saturday night. When the first city hall was built in 1924, it had a new jail with a barred window facing Broadway, and people could stop and see the prisoners through the bars.

In 1907, there was a shootout at the intersection of Market and Elm Streets. At that time, saloon keepers and their patrons had just about taken control of the city. The city marshal had a difficult time attempting to enforce new ordinances without help from the Wood and Hopkins County Sheriff's Departments. While the saloons brought people to town, and business to local merchants, they were places that fostered rowdy crowds and regular citizens were often reluctant to go on Market Street. Growing crime also became a serious problem. Shortly, many of the business people realized that it was time to enforce law and order on the Bowery.

In response to the need for some kind of control, the city employed the Wofford brothers, John as city marshal and Amos as a constable, to clean up the town. Tensions grew between the law enforcement officers and the saloon owners who didn't like them cracking down on illegal activity in the saloons.

One Saturday, February 3, 1907, at about 5:30 in the afternoon, John and Amos Wofford were standing in front of the barbershop on the corner of Elm and Market Streets, watching people come and go, most on their way home after doing Saturday shopping. The day appeared to be a peaceful Saturday, with few problems, until three or four men emerged from the Milam saloon and walked directly across the street toward John and Amos, who were in a conversation with Jim Gault.

Hostile words were exchanged and then they started pushing at each other. Soon they all drew their pistols, and gunshots rang in the air as some fifteen to eighteen shots were fired. It seems the Milam group fully intended to have a shootout with law enforcement officers. After the smoke cleared, the Wofford brothers and Dick and Bud Milam were lying in a sea of mud in the street. Shortly, all four shooters would be dead from the bullet wounds.

Today, all that remains of the shootout, which took place over 109 years ago, are the folklore tales which have been passed down from one generation to the next.

## A conspiracy?

In 1993, I visited with a friend whose father had witnessed the 1907 shootout while standing on the Market Street board sidewalk, observing the Saturday afternoon activities with two other men.

He said that the bullets that killed the Wofford brothers came from rifle fire out of the two-story structure across the street. That would have to have been the old First National Bank, which was remodeled in 1912. According to the story, rifle bullets were found near where the law officers fell during the onslaught. The Milam brothers had only been armed with pistols at the time of the shootout, according to documentation.

Other records indicate that the Hopkins County Sheriff attempted to contact John and Amos Wofford on the day of the shoot-out and inform them that a plot had been conceived to kill them. The Hopkins County Sheriff said he was sending a deputy to Winnsboro to offer help, but the deputy arrived too late. Wood County authorities also informed the law enforcement officers that a plot had been planned to get rid of them. But it appears the Wofford brothers did not show fear. They thought they were capable of handling the problem.

Yes, after more than one hundred years of stories, it is my opinion that a conspiracy was developed by saloon keepers, and maybe one or two disgruntled business owners, who hatched a plan to rid the community of John and Amos Wofford. Maybe at first, they just wanted to run them out of town, but it ended with the death of four people.

On May 13, 2002, after nearly one hundred years, the brave law enforcement officers John and Amos Wofford, who helped bring law in order to Texas, received their just dues when their names were inscribed on the marble walls of the National Law Enforcement Officers Memorial at Judiciary Square,

Washington D.C. These fallen officers will be forever honored and remembered.

## The end of The Bowery

By 1910, most of the virgin timber had been cut, and the large lumber producers moved their operations south. About the same time, all the saloons in Winnsboro had closed as a result of a local option election. The unruly element either cleaned up its act or moved on to the next Texas boomtown.

Some of the buildings that housed the saloons were lost in a devastating fire in 1940, when two of the buildings that had been at 206 and 208 Market Street. were totally destroyed. Three other buildings were slightly damaged. Over the years, the other buildings changed hands several times. The building on the corner of Market and Broadway that is now the Winnsboro Center For the Arts, encompasses two of the buildings, 200 and 202 Market Street. The corner building was once Massel saloon, and then it was a restaurant, then a grocery and feed store, a retail hardware store. It was an antique store before Mr. Al Stillman bought it and rented it to the Winnsboro Center for the Arts. Later, the art center purchased the building from Stillman, and it continues to operate at that location.

The other side of the art center, which was 202 Market Street, also began as a saloon and later became a grocery store. At one time, Skeen Bolding had a harness and shoe shop there. He also made saddles.

The building that now adjoins the art center, and currently houses Monk's Oven, a specialty pizza restaurant, may have housed a saloon, but there is no documentation of that. J. I. Connor is the first known owner of the building. He operated a successful grocery and produce business, shipping large lots of local produce by rail to markets in Dallas and beyond. When a customer entered Connor Grocery and Feed Company, they could see a small area to the left of the entrance that served as a shop for a tailor. Later, Hoodrow Melton, Sr. operated Melton Pharmacy there.

After many years of running his business, Connor retired in about 1925. He leased the building to Reba Harris, who operated Reba's Café for about twenty years. In 1945, Taft Tinney bought the building after Reba's Café closed. Tinney opened a business called Tinney Feed and Seed.

Taft was a local boy, born in 1908 near what is known today as Tinney Chapel Methodist Church. He grew up in Winnsboro and became a schoolteacher at Stout and then at Vernon, where he served as the principal.

Tinney was affiliated with the Winnsboro Farmers' Co-Op Association on East Elm and soon became a Purina Feed dealer. When he moved the business to 204 market Street, good things began to happen.

He was a pioneer in the poultry business, instrumental in organizing the Tri-County Broiler Association. In the late '50s and early '60s, Taft had more broiler chickens than Pilgrim did at Pittsburg. He furnished baby chicks and feed and hauled chickens to the processor in Tyler. Trouble started with the processing plant in Tyler when they did not send payment for the chickens on a timely basis. Taft began paying the chicken farmers out of his pocket so they could meet their financial obligations. One morning at 3:00 a.m., the truck driver who was taking a load of chickens to Tyler called and said the plant was padlocked. Apparently, the owner had filed bankruptcy and left town without letting anyone know. Taft had advanced growers about $60,000, which was a huge sum of money in 1960. He never asked growers to reimburse him or to take any responsibility for a part of the loss. He was a generous man his entire life, saying, "If it's mine, it's yours." He was known for his honesty and loyalty and his customers were faithful.

When Taft Tinney died in 1983, John Leaton acquired the building from the Tinney estate and used it primarily for storage purposes. In 2003, Al Stillman approached Mr. Leaton about donating the building to the Winnsboro Center for the Arts. Al explained the tax benefits to John, who at first said no, but Al convinced him to accept the proposal. After some discussions and adjustments, the property became a part of the art center thanks to the efforts of Stillman and members of the art center.

For the next ten years, the Winnsboro Center for the Arts used the building primarily for storage and their annual fund-raising garage sale, as they did not have capital to restore the structure. Finally, after much deliberation by the board of directors, the art center decided the building must be sold, on the condition they could find a buyer who had a love for

Market Street and a vested interest in Winnsboro. Prayers were answered when Shannon Monk shared plans for her business that would offer a nice improvement to Market Street and provide needed funds for renovation of the art center building.

In the fall of 2013, Mike and Shannon Monk, along with Shannon's brother, Scott Smith, bought the property at 204 Market St. from the art center. They began an immediate total restoration of the building, and the Winnsboro Center for the Arts began a renovation of their building. Both sites are now great attractions for the downtown Winnsboro area.

## Chapter Five - Notable People of Winnsboro

One late summer day in 2013, when I was visiting the Farmer's Market at City Park, I thought about the farmers of my youth who were called truck farmers. Franklin Street, between Locust and the packing shed at the depot in downtown Winnsboro, was filled by farmers, offering all kinds of vegetables for sale. Shippers would come by and offer maybe two dollars a bushel for a load of squash but the farmer would say, "Two thirty-five, or I feed them to my dogs."

This particular Saturday morning, while viewing the vegetables and visiting with friends, I ran into Roy Stout, who had all types of vegetables for sale. When Roy's ancestors arrived here in 1819, Indians still freely roamed the countryside. There were no towns, houses, bridges, or stores; only a few log cabins. His first ancestor to come to Texas was Henry Stout.

### Stout was overlooked by Texas historians

Texas historians, to my dismay, have overlooked the exploits of Henry Stout, whose Texas adventures would last for over seventy years. He served as a trusted friend of Sam Houston. Another friend, Davy Crockett, beat Stout in a shooting match—one of the few times he was ever bested by another shooter. About the only thing that has retained his name is the community of Stout, as well as Stout Creek.

On that warm Saturday morning in 2013, Roy Stout told me that he had received material about his famous ancestor that might interest me. "It's research you've never seen before," said Roy. "I'll send you a copy."

So, this is a page of Texas history that I have the honor of sharing with all of you. The date was July 1, 1887 in Fort Worth as Henry Stout, first sheriff of Wood County, was being interviewed by a reporter from the Weekly Gazette while at Union Station. Stout did not claim to be a resident of any town, and he belonged to a generation that had passed away. He was still tall and slender and active, his head covered by a full abundance of gray hair. His face was clean-shaven.

In this interview, Stout tells the reporter how he came to Fort Worth and had a layover while waiting for a train that would take him to Winnsboro. "There, yes, right down yonder, is that patch of woods where we passed in '41. I can follow that trail from here to where we buried John Denton (the man that Denton and Denton County are named for) thirty-eight years ago."

Memories clouded the old man's eyes.

With prompting by the Gazette reporter, the eighty-eight-year-old Stout continued his story. "I'm one of the old ones," he said. "When Sam Houston was about finishing up his business with the Mexicans, he left me to guard the frontier. General Houston knew me and knew if I was left there would be no Indian problems in the settlements. When the Mexican war was over, I went home and never received a discharge. I have been fighting Indians since 1819."

(On that particular day in 1887, Stout was returning from Austin after getting a settlement that could have been his Civil War allotment.)

The reporter reminded Stout that he had been saying something about finding the bones of Denton. The reporter was hoping to bring the story back to the stirring events of so long ago. Stout thought for a moment and then started to talk. "It cost me fifty cents for a place to sleep for three hours." Stout was referring to his current visit and the reporter pointed out that hotels charged fifty to seventy-five cents for a room regardless of the time occupied. In response, Stout said, "I never used to pay for a bed when I was here before. I slept on the prairie."

Once more the reporter reminded Stout that he'd been talking about finding Denton's grave, so Stout relayed the information. "How I came to look for Denton's bones was this way—Denton was killed in 1841. Many people had looked for his grave, but nobody could find it. Major Jarvis sent word for me to come to Fort Worth. This being thirty-eight years after the burying. I came to Major Jarvis's house and stopped for the night. Next morning, I was outfitted with the horse and some provisions and began the trip to locate Denton's remains. I rode along the skirt of timber northeast of Fort Worth. Before long, I struck the trail and remembered it as the one I traveled years before. We went up the forks of Fossil and Trinity near Birdville, the area's oldest settlement."

This was 1879, and the trail was worn by wagon wheels. The hills, woods, and rocks were still just as Stout had seen them through the eyes of memories for nearly forty years. The trail, unknown to others, was to him something that could not be taken away.

That scouting party was able to find the bones of John B. Denton. Stout had said "I knew where we buried him and it was near that old leaning tree."

When asked by one of the members of the scouting party just who was John B. Denton, the old man seemed astonished at the ignorance of the man who had asked the question and he answered, "John Denton was one of the grandest men Texas ever contained. He was a good and brave man. He used to be a circuit rider over in Arkansas and a powerful exporter. He came to Texas at an early age and studied law, preaching, farming, and fighting Indians. He was a pious man, and a truer friend and more daring spirit has never lived."

Denton's remains were later reburied on the grounds of the Denton County Courthouse in Denton, Texas.

Henry Stout related to the Gazette reporter some of Denton's life and history before he was killed. "We were living in Red River County growing our corn," Stout said, "and an Indian party came through and killed a whole family. (Stout was talking about the Ripley family massacre that happened east of Mount Vernon.) General Tarrant was there, but he did not order us out. We had a discussion among ourselves and elected Olen our captain. Tarrant was slighted but wanted to come along and offered to serve under anyone elected. I always thought Tarrant's blundering

## Reflections of Winnsboro

and cowardice was the cause of Denton's death, and I always will. Eventually Tarrant did succeed in getting himself elected to command and he got scared at the wrong time."

Stout continued his story, "We met eight miles north of Clarksville, near Pecan Point, and informed our company we knew where the Kechi village was in Wise County. We traveled by night to Bridgeport, on the Trinity, and found the village deserted. Then we went south on the Jack County line to the Brazos, hunting for the Indians until we ended up at the upper edge of the Cross Timbers at a big spring where we stayed the night." (This land area is north and northeast of present day Fort Worth.)

"The next day, we rode toward Birdbill, a small settlement with fortifications for protections from the Indians, then we went on to the forks of the Trinity and Fossil rivers where we made camp. This was the night before the fight. Tarrant said we should give up the chase and go back before the Trinity raised but it didn't look like rain. We could not agree. Although branded with cowardice, Tarrant concluded he would go along."

Next day, the search continued. "We followed a buffalo trail down to Fossil, then as we crossed the river, pony tracks were discovered and we saw the brush along the trail had been pulled out of grassy mounds of oats and rye. We knew we were close and sent word back to the main party. There were five men in this scouting party. The remainder of the army of seventy were behind under Tarrant. Denton was a member of the scouting party with me. We passed a knoll and ran into a whole tribe of Indians, but they didn't see us. We saw two squaws washing clothes. One of them had a baby in her arms.

"Because Tarrant had not committed his men, this scouting party of five was going it alone and we charged the camp. When we got within seventy-five yards, the squaws saw us. One ran to the creek, and the one with the baby ran toward me. I could've killed both. Thinking of the eight members of the Ripley family that had been murdered, it's a wonder I did not. But I let them go, and the Indians sought shelter. Me and Denton broke off from the other three scouts and went to a small ravine where ten to tweve Indians fired from the heavy growth alongside the ravine. I heard shots and looked at Denton who raised his rifle to shoot but dropped it and fell dead. I was struck in the arm and another bullet hit the stock of my rifle, tearing off the spring and knocking the stock against my head with such force I was stunned."

Stout showed the reporter his shattered and scarred arm and then said, "Tarrant heard the guns but never made a move to assist us. He sent a handful of men to look for Indians, knowing very well if we found them we would have to fight. As soon as one of the other scouts, Bowlin, heard the shooting, he rushed to our assistance. Another scout, Scott, shouted that Denton had been killed, and that I was wounded. Scott cursed the stupidity that brought the attack. I was bleeding profusely and Bowlin said we better return to the camp."

Toward the end of the interview by the Gazette reporter, Stout talked about the death of the famous Cherokee leader, Chief Bowles. "We did not do Bowles right, and I'll always regret it," Stout said. "Bowles was

# Reflections of Winnsboro

a friend of the white man. In 1836, when the report got out that Houston was whipped, some Indians wanted to whip us, but Bowles dissented. He told the others that while the Indians might whip a few frontiersmen, there were many other whites and too many to attack. I believe that he thus averted a war."

Later when Texas passed a law providing that no colored person could hold land, this applied to the Cherokees. The Indians were told to quit the country at an impossible time and when they explained they could not, they were told to give up their arms. Bowles was willing, but his braves rebelled and a fight ensued. This took place southwest of Tyler involving eight hundred Cherokee men women and children, who some historians said had only twenty-five guns against five hundred well-armed whites. The Cherokee war has been referred to by some historians as a massacre of the red man.

"Yes, we did Bowles wrong," repeated Stout before saying goodbye to the reporter and boarding the train that would carry him to his peaceful surroundings near Winnsboro.

Through the annals of history, few men have emerged as trailblazers, but Henry Stout personified the nineteenth-century American pioneer spirit. He was born in Logan County Virginia in 1799, moved to Illinois at a young age, and was raised among Indians. As a young man, he spent a year in Arkansas where he met and married Mary Talbot. In 1819, Henry and the family, which now included a son, James Selen, who was later known primarily by his middle name, migrated to Texas. They arrived in

Nacogdoches at the time of the unsuccessful Long Rebellion against the rule of Spain. Most Anglos in the area fled to Louisiana, but Henry would not leave until his corn was harvested.

In December of that year he began a journey to the north, through the wilderness of East Texas. He walked with nothing more than a blanket and a bag of parched corn, while Sarah and the boy rode horseback. The trip ended one hundred fifty miles later on the Red River near the Jonesboro Crossing, then part of Miller County, Arkansas. The inhabitants of the small community were the first human beings Stout had seen since leaving Nacogdoches.

During the 1820s, Henry Stout made his living as a scout, hunter, and guide, and by trading with the Indians. Sometime during this period Stout established a camp at the forks of the Delaware Creek near a spring at the location of present-day Clarksville. A tribe of Delaware Indians also share this ground, and other tribes of Caddo, Kickapoo, and Shawnee Indians also occupied land in this territory; there is no evidence Stout had any serious problems with them.

Henry built a log cabin and opened a trading post at that location and later would receive a deed of land at this site from the Republic of Texas. When the transaction became effective in 1837, Stout transferred the title to the family of James Clark, who established the town of Clarksville that bears his name. In the early 1830s, Henry joined Gen. Thomas Rusk, James Clark, John Stiles, and a party of United States representatives on the Red River above Jonesboro for the purpose of making peace and getting a treaty with unfriendly Indians. It seems that Stout Knew Indian Chief

Cuthand and played a role in helping to bring about the treaty.

It must've been around 1830 or 1831, when Henry Stout met Sam Houston. I have heard that he became acquainted with Houston when the future hero of San Jacinto was living with the Cherokee Indians in Eastern Oklahoma. I do know that when Houston was on his way to Texas, he traveled to Fort Towson and the Red River crossing at Jonesboro.

During the latter part of 1835, Davy Crockett crossed the Red River at Jonesboro and spent time with his old friend, John Stiles, at the White Rock community northwest of present-day Clarksville. Stiles was a cousin of Daniel Boone and had been friends with Crockett back in Tennessee. Crockett wanted to go on a buffalo hunt for the sport and to acquire meat for his group of Tennessee volunteers. Stout agreed to lead the party on the expedition. Crockett's horses were exhausted from the trip from Tennessee, so it became necessary to borrow fresh mounts. The hunting party traveled west for nearly one hundred miles searching for buffalo. It is not known if they were successful, but there was one interesting event. While riding their horses around the edge of a wooded area, where the grass reached the horses bellies, they suddenly found themselves surrounded by hives of ground bees. Crockett wrote to his family in Tennessee that when this trip was over he would like to return and settle in this "Honey Grove." Later, Crockett's friends settled there and officially named the community Honey Grove.

## General calls for help

General Sam Houston took command of the Texas Revolutionary Army on March 11, 1836 and immediately sent word to his Red River friends to join him in the coming battle with Mexico. Henry Stout would serve with Capt. William Becknall's company of the Calvary brigade under Gen. Thomas J. Rusk. After the fall of the Alamo, the "Red River Boys" traveled as fast as possible to join General Houston during his retreat from Gonzales to near Harrisburg prior to the Battle of San Jacinto.

This is speculation on my part, but it is my belief that when Stout arrived on the scene, Houston sent his trusted friend on a scouting mission to determine the exact locations of the Mexican army. The historic battle that won Texas its independence took place on April 21, 1836, near what is now the city of Houston.

Mexican General Santa Anna managed to escape from the battle of San Jacinto, but was captured the following day. According to Stout family records, Houston summoned Henry, who had received the leg wound during the battle, and requested his help in picking the man who would guard and protect the Mexican leader. Santa Anna's life had been threatened by members of the Citizens Army. Stout himself could not serve as a guard because of his leg wound, but recommended the selection of his son Selen, along with John Stiles and another soldier whose name is not known.

## Returning home

After the war ended and the Treaty of Velasco was signed, Stout and the other Red River volunteers returned to their homes. His son, Selen, would serve as a scout for the Texas Revolutionary Army from July to October 1836.

Henry received an appointment as captain and commanding officer of the Red River Rangers in 1838. It should be noted that those rangers were not part of the Texas Rangers as we know them today. They were minutemen, formed to protect settlers and handle other dangers along the frontier.

Ultimately, Henry Stout settled in what is now Wood County. When Stout came to East Texas, I surmise, he was looking for a tame, more gentle and peaceful place to live. He had spent more than twenty-five years in Texas fighting outlaws, the Mexican army, Indians, and wild animals. He had received a number of serious arrow and bullet wounds, not to mention scars from tangling with five-hundred-pound bears with nothing but a skinning knife to protect himself.

After many years of frontier living, Stout seem to prosper in Wood County. He became a successful farmer and constructed a gristmill, using water from the stream on his property as power. He dammed the creek, constructed a mill run, and when sufficient water had accumulated, it ran the mill until the water was so low that it did not provide the necessary energy. Using this method, Stout could grind approximately two hundred fifty pounds of cornmeal each day.

He also established a freight hauling business, running wagons from Jefferson to settlements in the West. It was during a Jefferson trip that one of his wagons became stuck in the middle of the stream. The water had been rising due to heavy rain. Stout demonstrated his great strength by carrying two-hundred-pound barrels of flour to dry ground through the raging water; thus saving the cargo. Henry Stout was elected the first sheriff of Wood County in 1850. He served with distinction in that office for two terms and outlaws stayed out of Wood County during his time as Sheriff. After his second term ended, Stout retired to his home in East Point, but soon he would be called to represent Wood and Van Zandt counties in the House of Representatives during the Sixth Texas Legislature from 1855 to 1856. When that term as state representative ended, Stout was ready to come home to Wood County. The political life of Austin and his store-bought clothes did not sit well with the frontiersman. He was more comfortable sleeping under the stars and wearing buckskin.

After serving in the Confederate Army from October 1861 to May 25, 1862, Stout returned to Wood County to live out his remaining years. Instead of retiring to his front porch and a rocking chair, Stout still had the robust actions of the frontiersman. He would put on exhibitions of his riding and shooting abilities, while lying down on the horse's neck with his gun hidden beneath his chest. Racing at full speed, and firing as he rode, Stout would hit targets that had been pointed out. One story relates an incident when Henry had a spat with his wife. Without saying a word, he picked up the wooden water bucket, walked out of the house to the spring, filled the bucket with water, hung the bucket on a tree limb—and walked away. Months later, he returned with a new bucket, scooped it full of water, and went back into the house. I don't know how the story ended, but I imagine that Henry's wife may have said a few choice words.

It was during a period of severe weather, and after a day of hard work, that he contracted pneumonia in 1892 and died at the age of ninety-three. A Texas historical marker was erected in a roadside park built by the Texas Department of Transportation, next to the Stout Cemetery located east of the East Point community on Farm to Market Road 2088.

## Continuing the legacy

Henry Stout's son, Selen, joined his father as a soldier and Texas Ranger, and he was a trusted scout for Gen. Sam Houston. In 1842, he led the Hargrove brothers from Clarksville to present-day Hopkins County on the South Sulphur River (Sulphur Bluff). Selen is acknowledged by historians as the one who led the first party of settlers into what is now known as Hopkins County. In 1841, Selen received 1,476 acres of land from his uncle, William Stout, and this frontier settlement was eight to nine miles north of present-day Winnsboro, originally known as Stout's Creek neighborhood. It was established four to five years before Hopkins County was organized in 1846 and was the beginning of a community later known as Pine Forest.

It is believed that Selen and his wife, Elvira Ritchie, must have established a residence here in the early 1840s. Selen developed an active business, acquiring and buying and selling land. He encouraged families to settle in the community and to establish roads, a church, and a school. He served on a committee to construct a road from Tarrant, then the county seat, to Mount Pleasant, and to review and mark a route from the bridge on White Oak Creek east of the boundary line of Hopkins County.

On October 12, 1861, at the age of forty-three, Selen enlisted, along with two sons, John and Benjamin, in Company F, 9th Texas Infantry, CSA. Selen served as a sergeant in the Confederate Army, his sons as privates. After the war, Selen and Elvira remained at Pine Forest for the remainder of their lives. They raised eleven children and are remembered as good citizens and community leaders.

## The Little Dutchman

Often, I think about a friendly little man with a strange accent who wandered the streets of Winnsboro for more than forty years. People found him amusing and most children formed a friendship with him that would last throughout life. This man, who was small in stature, might be described as the Pied Piper of Winnsboro. He loved children and he loved Scouting. I'm sure he never had much more than twenty dollars in his pocket at any one time, but he would always offer small children money for a cold drink, candy, or a

**Reflections of Winnsboro**

show ticket. His full name was John Christian Kruger, but everyone called him Dutch.

Dutch was born about 1879 in Holland and went to sea at the age of fourteen as a cabin boy on the Brennen. The ship docked at Hoboken, New Jersey, and the following day a fire erupted in the harbor. Dutch saved two young children from the blaze, and because of this heroic deed, U.S. immigration officials allowed him to remain in this country.

This young immigrant went to work at St. Mary's Hospital in Hoboken as an orderly. He soon learned to speak a little English and write his name, however his strong native accent would remain throughout his life. After number of other jobs that included working as a gardener, and in a carnival, and the aluminum mine at Bauxite, Arkansas, he came to Texas.

In 1922, Dutch arrived in Winnsboro with the Cannady Carnival as the operator of the ferris wheel and the merry-go-round. The carnival set up on a large vacant lot known as the cotton yard behind the First Assembly of God Church on Locust Street. When the carnival left two weeks later, the ferris wheel operator decided to stay in Winnsboro for a while. For a number of years, he worked as a handyman, mowed yards, cleaned buildings, and worked at the produce market. He eventually became a house painter and paperhanger, and that's when things began to improve for him. He also worked for the Kraft Cheese Company for many years.

The wit and wisdom of Dutch began to attract the curiosity of local children. This folklore storyteller began to entertain kids with tales of the South seas, shipwrecks, and the people he met while working for the Wild West show. He talked about being acquainted with Buffalo Bill Cody, as well as the famous Indians who were part of the show. Some of those fascinating stories may have been a bit fictional, but we never questioned old Dutch.

If there's one thing Dutch would like to be remembered for, it would be his association with the Boy Scouts of America. He helped organize the local Boy Scout troops in 1924 and became a Scoutmaster of Troop One. Later he was Scoutmaster of Troop 392 and Troop 379. Dutch always referred to the scouts as his boys.

Each summer in the 1940s and '50s, Winnsboro Boy Scouts joined about a dozen other troops for a week's encampment at Camp Tonkawa for a week of swimming, merit badge classes, and military-type training. Scouts lived in tents and ate in a mess hall, and the cost for this week of adventure was seven dollars and fifty cents. Most of us had summer jobs that helped pay for the week of fun.

At night, there was always a large bonfire, and all members of Winnsboro Troop 392 would sit on the ground around the fire and listen to the stories related by Dutch. Often members of other troops would join us at the fire to also listen to the stories. Dutch had a remarkable memory of scouts from the 1920s, '30s, and '40s; those who served in the military during World War II; scouts who lost their lives in the war; and those whose fathers were scouts in one of Dutch's troops. Dutch would always end the evening by playing beautiful music on his worn accordion.

# Reflections of Winnsboro

During the week of camp, pranks were always a part of the outing. One prank that was long remembered was a letter that was sent from Camp Tonkawa to Miss Elizabeth Souter asking her for a date. We signed the letter Dutch Kruger. Thankfully, both Dutch and Miss Souter were goods sports and laughed about our silly prank.

After a week of busy activities, a tired, sunburned, and homesick group of kids would begin the trip back home. It was always a good week; meeting scouts from other towns and learning the art of survival and what military life would be like in a few years for most of us, but for now everyone was glad to be going home.

Dutch was elected to the Order of the Arrow, one of Scouting's most prestigious honors. In 1957, the grateful people of Winnsboro passed the hat and raised enough money to send him to the National Boy Scout Jamboree in Valley Forge Pennsylvania to receive his award.

This fascinating little man was also very instrumental in organizing Little League sports. At the dedication of Lyons Park in 1957, he made the following comment, "Thanks to the people of Winnsboro for letting me have their children, for I have had more joy out of their children than the children did out of me."

Dutch died on July 9, 1966 at the age of 87. Although he passed without any surviving family, he had the largest family in town. The first Baptist Church was filled with young and old Scouts and Scout executives from all parts of East Texas, as well as many residents of the city, who all loved and respected this man. If John Christian Kruger is looking down on Winnsboro today, I am sure he is happy to know "his kids" still think of him.

# Chapter Six - Wood County Notable Citizens

Wood County had many outstanding citizens through the years, and none identified more with the county than James Stephen Hogg and his daughter Ima. Stories about Jim and Ima were passed on to me by two friends, the late M. D. Carlock and Eddie Spacek, father of Sissy Spacek. Eddie and M. D. were special friends of Miss Ima Hogg. She often stayed in their homes while visiting Wood County, and both men knew a lot about the legacy of her and her father.

Jim Hogg was the first native-born Texan to hold the state's highest office, and he is remembered as one of Texas's greatest governors. Even President Harry Truman considered him one of America's greatest governors.

Jim Hogg was born on March 24, 1851 at Mountain home, the plantation home of his parents near Rusk. In 1862, his father, Joseph, a general in the Confederate Army, died while commanding troops during the Civil War. The following year, his mother died of an unknown disease believed to be consumption. After the outstanding family debts had been paid, young Jim became a penniless orphan.

Andrew Jackson, publisher of the Rusk Observer, was fond of Jim. He taught the boy to set type and hired him as a printer's devil at the newspaper. (A printer's devil was a person, typically a young boy, serving at or below the level of apprentice in a printing establishment.) Time passed, and in the fall of 1867, this rather strange-looking young man walked up the road from Mineola to Quitman. He looked like a sixteen-year-old boy, but he was larger in size than most of the men in town. He walked barefoot, with his shoes across his left shoulder, while a bundle of clothes hung from his right shoulder.

He entered the newspaper office of the Quitman Clipper and approached Doc Shuford, who was editor and publisher, and inquired about a job. There were no openings, but Doc felt sorry for the hungry-looking boy, who had no job, and took him on as an apprentice. Salary consisted of room and board and clothing, so Jim often took any odd jobs he could find to make money. He liked Quitman, and the people there liked him, and before long he became owner and publisher of the Quitman News.

In 1873, this self-educated man with a burning desire to succeed became Justice of the Peace, Wood County, Precinct 1. He had a great interest in legal matters and began to read books on the meaning of law. W. M. Giles of Mineola often loaned him books from his law library. Hogg also made frequent trips to Gilmer to meet with O. M. Roberts, a learned lawyer who later served as governor of Texas from 1879 to 1883. After reading law for four years, Jim passed the state bar exam in 1875 and quickly became a well-prepared lawyer who didn't back down from anyone.

His frequent trips to Gilmer were not altogether of a business nature, as Jim had become acquainted with a charming young lady named Sallie Stinson, daughter of

James Stinson, a prominent Wood County farmer who lived south of Little Hope at Holly Springs. Jim would arrange to be in the vicinity of the Stinson home usually about mealtime.

Sallie and Jim were married at the Stinson home in 1874 and four children were born to this union: Will, Mike, Thomas, and Ima. Ima was born in Mineola and would become Wood County's, and the state's, beloved Miss Ima. Governor Connolly designated Miss Ima as Texas's unofficial goodwill ambassador.

In 1878, Jim Hogg became County Attorney for Wood County, then two years later became District Attorney for the Seventh Judicial District of Texas. Hogg prosecuted criminals without fear or favor but barely escaped the vengeance of the outlaw element on several occasions. After serving as district attorney, Jim opened a law office in Tyler and soon became leader of the Smith County Democratic Party. In 1886, he was elected Attorney General of Texas and began prosecuting lawbreakers. The first to receive Hogg's judicial wrath were illegal insurance companies. Next, the giant railroad conglomerates were forced to comply with Texas laws.

In 1891, James Stevens Hogg was inaugurated Governor of Texas. His reign as governor might be described as one in which rich and poor alike were compelled to obey the laws of Texas. After two terms as governor, a tired Jim Hogg, now with health problems, retired from public service. Sallie died in 1895, following an illness, leaving Jim heartbroken.

During his years serving Texas as Attorney General, and then governor, Jim Hogg often stepped on the toes of "white-shirt lawbreakers." Now, upon leaving the Governor's mansion in Austin, Jim found himself naturally poor as he had never accepted bribes during his many years of public office. He had gone to Austin without great wealth and returned home about the same. However, he did not die poor—oil was discovered on his East Texas land and he had his law practice in Houston and Austin. Jim Hogg died in 1906 and is buried in the Oakwood Cemetery in Austin.

Over the years, Hogg visited Winnsboro frequently, meeting with old friends M. D. Carlock Sr. and W. R. McGill, a Winnsboro lawyer.

Ima Hogg and her brothers were Texas philanthropists who spent millions of dollars restoring landmarks throughout the state. Once, while a houseguest of Mr. Carlock Jr. she said, "M. D., I would like to do more for Wood County, but I just don't have the money."

In 1999, I had the honor of presiding over a ceremony at the site where Miss Ima was born in Mineola in 1882. We dedicated a Texas historical marker to commemorate her and all of the things that she did for the state of Texas.

## Virginia Bozeman

Several women have played important roles in the growth and development of Winnsboro throughout history. However, it would be impossible to imagine anyone who worked more diligently to bring intellectual understanding the youth of this community then Mrs. T. U. Bozeman. For over forty years, the names of Carnegie Library and Mrs. Bozeman were synonymous, as this friend of Winnsboro personified all that is wonderful about a library.

Virginia was born in Hunt County on October 25, 1873, the daughter of David and Rachel Boyd, a prominent Greenville family. After completing high school, she attended Baylor University, and in 1903 Virginia met Titus U. Bozeman. They married in 1904 and moved to Winnsboro, where Titus worked for Perkins Brothers, the largest dry goods store in Winnsboro. Perkins Brothers was located at 107 East Elm. In about 1918, Titus became the store manager and served in that capacity until his death in 1934. The Bozeman family lived in a comfortable home at 300 West Broadway, which is now the site of Davis chiropractic.

Books were the constant companion of Virginia Byrd Bozeman when she awakened each morning and retired each night. It might be proper to say that "Bunny", as her friends called her, understood the meaning of what was hidden between the pages of books in addition to just words.

In 1908, Mayor R. B. Howell and banker Charles Morris persuaded the Carnegie Foundation to contribute $10,000 for a public library. The grant stipulated that the library must be wholly supported by the community. The city acquired a library site at South Main and West Broadway (Carnegie), which now houses an auto parts store.

The large imposing building, with the wide steps and massive columns, was completed in 1909, with the bottom floor used as an auditorium and opera house known as Carnegie Hall, while the upper floor housed the library. Citizens were proud of this magnificent edifice of knowledge. It was one of the finest buildings in East Texas, but the city did not have the financial means to furnish the showplace. Mayor Howell and Mr. Morris acquired bookshelves, tables, and chairs from merchants, but the library contained less than two hundred books. The only lighting came from kerosene lamps until hardware merchant J. E. McBride donated a hanging gas lamp.

On September 6, 1910, the Standard Club sponsored a book donation and opened the library to book lending. The club selected Mrs. Bozeman, who had been a member of the organization since 1904, as the librarian, with a salary of ten dollars per month. By 1933, the salary increased to twenty-five dollars monthly. She scanned every book to determine proper content, which eventually became thousands, before placing them on the shelves. She boasted that no objectionable books found their way into hands of young readers.

For several years, the Standard Club sponsored an annual flower show, with proceeds going to the library fund, and in recent years the club has depended largely on donations from the annual coffee benefit to aid the financial needs of the library. Members of the Standard Club, both present and past, are to be congratulated for their dedication to this worthy project which has raised thousands of dollars since 1910.

Children of past generations recall going to the library in search of material for research papers, and that never represented a problem as Mrs. Bozeman knew exactly where to locate needed information. She was a walking encyclopedia, a staunch disciplinarian from the old school, especially within the confines of the library. When a young patron entered the space, he or she would gently cross the squeaking floor. If a youngster had a word for a pal, they spoke in a whisper when Mrs. Bozeman was not looking. If she did catch them visiting, she would remind them that the library was the place to study, not talk. A one-sentence profile of Mrs. Bozeman might read something like this; "She looked like a librarian and acted like a librarian."

By the late 1940s, Winnsboro's devoted librarian started to show the accumulation of her years. She walked slower to her treasure house of learning each morning, and Mrs. Connie Craddock, the assistant librarian, began to assume most of the responsibilities. Then in 1951, poor health forced Mrs. Bozeman to retire from the post she had held since 1910 and Mrs. Craddock became the librarian.

Still, Bunny maintained her love for books and spent most of her time reading. When her health permitted, she attended services at First Baptist Church and occasionally taught Sunday school. She died August 19, 1954, and she was laid to rest beside her husband at Lee Cemetery. If the Lord had extended one last wish to Mrs. Bozeman, I feel sure the request would have been for five minutes more to examine the next page of the book she had been reading.

Unfortunately, the old Carnegie library building was torn down. The city sold the land to Berkshires Food Stores to open a grocery store in town. Funds from that sale were used to build another library site at 200 West Broadway. Many people in the community were saddened to see the old building destroyed.

Jumping ahead to 1985, when the estate of Fern Gilbreath made $60,000 available to build a library, Judge T. C. Chadick donated land for the new library at 916 North Main. Because of the keen interest in having a better library building, area citizens got busy, rolled up their sleeves, and began a massive fund raiser. Soon available funds for a new library reached $687,000, and in 1986, the city received a grant of $100,000 toward the building. In September 1986, construction began on the 606,000-square-foot building that was to be known as the Gilbreath Memorial Library. The dreams of many library patrons was becoming a reality.

If Mrs. Bozeman is looking down on the same today, I'm sure she would be feeling humbled to be remembered, as well as by the success of her beloved library through the diligence of many library patrons over the last 114 years.

## More about Fern Gilbreath

The Gilbreath family settled here soon after Texas became a state, and they were successful farmers. In the 1930s, Fern became the local Conoco distributor for oil and gas products. His office and distribution center was where Bill Coe's oil and gasoline business is today. He maintained a service station located where the telephone exchange is today on North Main.

The family of John Crow ran the gas station for year, and Mr. Gilbreath and Bose Mikule, owner of a bakery, constructed a croquet court on the lot west of the station. It had outdoor lights, and men often

## Reflections of Winnsboro

congregated on the lot until 9:00 or 9:30 at night. In the 1930s and 1940s, croquet was a gentleman's sport.

During those years, Fern Gilbreath, in his quiet way, was involved in most civic and church-related activities. Fern's wife was Fanny K. Williams, daughter of Moody Williams, who owned a blacksmith shop on Franklin Street that later became Winnsboro's largest plumbing business.

Fern received a limited education, but by 1922, he had become a brilliant self-educated man and publisher of a small newspaper, The Sunday Topic, which was produced every Saturday by the print shop. The newspaper office was located in the alley at the rear of the Rhone building, now a part of the First National Bank of Winnsboro drive-thru and parking lot on West Elm. Gilbreath said his job involved everything from reporting, office manager, typesetter, publisher, then delivering free copies all over town.

The small journal was supported by area churches who offered a membership directory and listing of weekly church activities in each edition. Local businesses also provided financial support through advertising, and the First National Bank, the only business still in existence today, was one of those early advertisers.

There were many interesting stories and headlines from The Sunday Topic in 1922, including one titled "Ain't it The Truth." The story read, "An old covered wagon went through Shawnee, Oklahoma the other day, and the wagon sheet bore this roughly inscribed explanation: Texas is starvation, Oklahoma is speculation, New Mexico is desperation, the whole world is shot to Hades with the Harding administration. I'm going back to Arkansas."

## Red Hightower

Lieutenant Colonel Louis Hightower, known as "Red" in his hometown of Winnsboro, was a hero in World War II. When a German 88mm shell fragment screamed down the tube of his own 70mm tank, tearing out the underside, Hightower ordered his crew to "git," and they escaped the burning hulk of the tank, dodging behind the Sherman and keeping it between them and five attacking German Mark IV Tanks.

Hightower had affectionately named his tank Texas, and afterward he commented that, "They even shot the Lone Star Flag from the antenna."

"Yeah," said the crewmembers, "but if the Colonel was going out to bid the devil 'good morning' the whole gang would go along and say 'howdy' too."

For his gallantry and bravery, Hightower received the Distinguished Service Cross for "extraordinary heroism, self-sacrifice, and devotion to duty worthy of the finest tradition of the Armed Forces and deserving of the highest praise."

Hightower also received high praise from a reporter at the Baltimore Sun, with one quote that read, "Tank Texas belongs in great tales of a hero facing overwhelming odds against the Mark IV, the mightiest German tank. The convoy owes their lives to Lieut. Col. Louis Hightower and his men."

In June 1943, Look Magazine featured a double-page layout and photograph of Hightower and his crew with the caption: "These brave soldiers make patriotic Americans proud."

Colonel Hightower joined his mentor, General Patton, for the remaining African Campaign. Patton spearheaded the American thrust that won the war in Africa and Red shared in the final battle and the muddy glory of victory. It was on the desert, and in the hills of Tunisia, Algeria, and along the Moroccan coast, that the United States learned through hard experience how to fight the Nazis. What was learned in Africa would pay big dividends in the invasion of Sicily, Italy, and France in June 1944.

During the Italy campaign, Hightower received a second Silver Star for gallantry while in action. Colonel Hightower was traveling with the forward tank element, and, with complete disregard for his own safety, he moved into the lead of the advancing tanks. He was several hundred yards ahead of the lead tank, sometimes walking and sometimes riding on top of the lead tank, until he was wounded when the tank sustained a hit from an antitank gun.

Seven years later, Hightower was in the heat of the battle in Korea. By then, he was a major general, and he was awarded a Bronze Oak Leaf Cluster for "exceptionally meritorious conduct in performance of outstanding service to the government of the United States."

My friend M. D. Carlock said that he and Red were friends as youths who fished and hunted together, went swimming in the mud holes around Winnsboro, and courted the local girls. Carlock referred to Red as a typical boy who never flaunted his brilliance. His father, Dr. Louis Hightower, a well-respected Winnsboro dentist, practiced his profession here for many years. Several times while I visited at the Carlock home, the phone would ring and it would be Red calling from Washington, D.C. M. D.s eyes would glimmer and a big smile would come across his face as they relived memories of yesteryear. In about 1994 or 1995, Red called M. D. from Walter Reed Hospital where Red was a patient. They talked for a while, and then all too soon Mr. Carlock and General Hightower were called home.

## Texas Troubadours

One day, in about the year 2005, while I was having coffee with the members of the Over the Hill Gang, I entered into a conversation with my friend, Curtis Rhoades, about his days as proprietor of a local eating establishment. The Rhoades Café was a clean family-style restaurant with the capacity to serve fifty patrons. He offered good food and good service at a reasonable price. I asked Curtis if he remembered serving a hot steak sandwich that included bread, chicken fried steak, and cream potatoes with gravy. When he answered yes, I accused him of overcharging, as this complete meal cost thirty-five cents in 1948.

We had a good laugh over that.

In 1948, the Winnsboro high school did not have a cafeteria. During the noon hour students either ate a sack lunch, walked home for lunch, or ate at their favorite restaurant. Rhoades Café had a large school-lunch business.

While we were reminiscing, Curtis asked me if I remembered when the Texas Troubadour, Ernest

**Reflections of Winnsboro**

Tubbs, came to Winnsboro. This was before my time, and before Tubbs became a star at the Grand Ole Opry. Curtis said that Tubbs made an appearance one Saturday afternoon near the intersection of Elm and Franklin Streets which was then known as Smoky Row. Tubbs stood in front of the Black Cat Café, playing music as a publicity event for a flour milling company in Fort Worth, Burris Mills.

Curtis said that on that Saturday afternoon, less than a dozen folks stopped to hear Tubbs play his guitar and sing. However, a few years later, millions of people would turn on their radios and televisions to listen to, and watch, Tubbs perform at the Grand Ole Opry on Saturday nights.

The Light Crust Doughboys also represented the Burris Mills in Fort Worth, and they frequently performed in Winnsboro in the 1930s and 1940s. Three of the earliest members of the band were Bob Wills, later known as the "King of Western Swing," Roy Rogers, and W. Lee O'Daniel, known as "Pappy the Flour Salesman."

O'Daniel used this exposure that made his name well-known to run for and win the governorship of Texas in 1938. Later he was elected a U.S. senator from Texas.

The Burris Mills Milling Company purchased a custom-built bus for the Doughboys to use in their travels. It was equipped with a portable generator and public address system, and an open platform at the back was used as a stage. Huge signs on the sides of the bus advertised Light Crust Flour and the Doughboys. The band played for events in places that ranged from remote communities and small hamlets to county fairs and commencement programs, always donating their services and musical talents. Everywhere the Doughboys performed, they were treated as special guests and the sale of Light Crust Flour soared.

# Chapter Seven – Schools & Places of Knowledge

## A pioneer in Texas education

John Creighton Buchanan was born in Greenwood, Louisiana in 1850. His family moved to Rusk County first and then later up to Gilmer, where he received a subscription-school education from the famous Professor Looney, an outstanding nineteenth-century Gilmer educator. Buchanan received certification to teach, and his first post was in Louisiana, where he also studied law. In 1873, Buchanan took the bar exam and was admitted to the Texas bar. That same year he established a law practice in Quitman.

In 1876, with a successful law practice, Buchanan was elected Wood County Attorney. The following year, he married Sarah Rosalie Patten, daughter of Dr. A. L. Patten, and the couple established a home in Mineola. After throwing his hat into the political ring, Buchanan was elected to the Texas State Senate from the 10th District, representing Wood, Van Zandt, Kaufman, Rains, Rockwall, and Hunt counties.

Following the stormy years of the Civil War and Reconstruction Period, Buchanan went to Austin in January 1879. Texas had little money to enact legislation for building roads, economic growth, education, or to pay salaries of state employees. As a junior member of the Sixteenth Texas Legislature, Buchanan was fortunate to draw a four-year term and would not have to stand for reelection until 1882. At the beginning of the seventeenth session in 1881, he emerged as a voice for the people, especially in matters of education. He became the chair of the Senate Committee of Educational Affairs and he authored the bill that established the University of Texas at Austin and the University's medical branch at Galveston.

In 1882, Buchanan easily won reelection for another two-year term. During that term, he authored a bill that established common school districts in Texas. The bill provided for a state superintendent for education, a county superintendent, and determined that all teachers must be certified by a board appointed by a county judge. Common school districts required schools to be open five days each week with no less than twenty school days per month. The bill divided each county into districts and gave individual counties the authority to levy local property taxes to fund the schools. Each district was managed by three elected trustees. For the first time, the legislation put control of public schools into the hands of local communities.

Sen. Buchanan led the charge to reform Texas public schools and devise a system for proper education; many of these principles remain in effect today as part of the Texas education system.

John Creighton Buchanan died December 9, 1884, at the age of thirty-four. He is buried in Mineola's City Cemetery. The Texas Historic Commission placed a Texas Historical Marker at the graveside, recognizing the pioneer achievements of Senator Buchanan in the field of education.

Rosa Buchanan, wife of Senator Buchanan and a longtime educator, received an appointment as Texas's first female appointee to a professorship at Sam Houston State University. She served in that position for a number of years, and when she retired, the university named one of its halls for her. Rosa returned to her beloved Mineola and died in 1941.

I was part of an historical event held in 1999 in Mineola that was sponsored by the Wood County Historical Commission. The event recognized and honored the achievements of John and Rosa Buchanan. Both left an important legacy to Wood County and Texas education.

## School days

Public education arrived at a snail's pace in Texas. During the administration of Governor Pease in 1854, the Texas Legislature enacted legislation to support education, but financial help was not available to school districts until after the civil war in about 1870. Prior to that, subscription schools offered the only means of education for most Texas children. However, early settlers were more interested in survival than book learning.

Here in East Texas, the first houses of learning were tuition schools. Few actual school buildings existed, so most classes were conducted in private homes or public buildings such as churches. One teacher usually offered instruction to all the students, who might number between thirty and forty children. One class would be instructed and how to decipher, another class studied spelling, and others were examining history. Most early teachers had little formal education, but if they could read and write, they were qualified to teach.

Tuition payment was in the form of syrup, sweet potatoes, hams, and lodging for the teacher. Since very little hard currency was available, barter represented the common form of exchange.

Winnsboro's first subscription school opened in 1857 near North Main and West Pine, with approximately twenty-five students meeting on the first floor of the Masonic Lodge Hall. Each semester consisted of a three- to four-month term.

Sometime in the late 1870s, Winnsboro Masonic Lodge (AF&AM No. 146) built a two-story Lodge building at the southwest corner of South Broadway (Carnegie) and Chestnut Streets. The lower floor was used as a school, opera house, church, and meeting house, while the upper floor served as Masonic Lodge Hall and meeting place. Isham Russell is said to be the first teacher at that site.

Traveling performers would arrive by train, put on a one- or two-night show in the opera house, and then move on to the next town.

In 1880, Winnsboro Baptists began construction of a sanctuary near Peach and Blackjack Streets, but money for completing the project was not available. Since the city had the responsibility to employ teachers, provide facilities, and offer education to Winnsboro youth, officials offered financial help to the church for completing the building with the stipulation that the sanctuary could be used for educational purposes. This is the first instance I found showing that public funds were used to support education in Winnsboro. Students not living within the city boundaries began seeking permission to attend school here, and city population experienced rapid growth.

In 1888, the city purchased land west of Walker Park and built a two-story school building, with four classrooms on the first floor and a study hall on the upper floor. Texas Collegiate Institute was a modern, Victorian structure with desks, blackboards, large windows, wood heaters in each room, and an elevated desk for teachers. The study hall served as the town's community center for meetings and social activities, as well as an election center.

The city of Winnsboro's Board of Education hired a new superintendent in 1902. J. P. Massey came to the city with ideas about education and how a school should be run to meet standards for affiliation with the University of Texas, but we were not ready for this rapid change. He advocated advanced studies, a nine-month school year, additional equipment, more classrooms for students, and holding a graduation ceremony. Massey spent only one year in Winnsboro as superintendent, and perhaps it was because he might have been ahead of his time, seeking such rapid educational changes.

W. S. Burks is given credit for conducting the first formal graduating class at Texas Collegiate Institute in about 1904. The date cannot be verified, but Aunt Lula Moore wrote in her memoirs that she attended the ceremony in 1904.

As student enrollment continued to grow, the city decided to sell the existing school property and move to a more central location. In 1905, they voted a $16,000 bond for a new facility but the bonds were not salable as the town had a weak tax base. That's when R. G. Andrews bought the bonds and built a school building on East Pine Street. It was a beautiful three-story building constructed of the finest material. It had eight classrooms on the first and second floors and a study hall on the third floor.

By 1910, state education requirements indicated that schools needed more teachers and additional classroom space to be a certified Texas school. J. H. Sheppard, an experienced educator, was hired as superintendent in Winnsboro. He was welcomed by a strong and well-qualified Board of Education, and Winnsboro now had a healthy tax base with which to support an additional school. Mr. Sheppard and the school board acquired land in the south part of town where Memorial Middle School is located today, and plans were drawn up to build a modern high school. The first eleventh-grade graduation was held in 1912. With two modern school buildings constructed within seven years, and a staff of experienced teachers, Winnsboro emerged as an outstanding East Texas education center, led by Superintendent Sheppard, who represented excellence in education for twenty-two years.

The old Dunbar school was built in the Black community east of town in 1927, and consisted of one room with a porch on the north side. A water keg on the porch supplied drinking water, and a woodstove provided heat. The school was named for Paul Dunbar, a Black nineteenth- to early twentieth-century poet and writer who gained national prominence for his work. The funding for this school came from the foundation established by Chicago millionaire Julius

Rosenwald, president of Sears Roebuck and Company. This was the third Black school in Winnsboro, and it served the community's educational needs until 1965. Two teachers in particular, Fannie Mae Wright and Ernestine Starling, influenced the lives of several generations of Dunbar students.

On October 26, 2002, Winnsboro School District held an event proclaiming it as Judge T. C. Chadick Day. It was a fitting tribute to an outstanding alumnus who excelled in both education and sports. Judge Chadick never faltered, whether in Austin or Washington, in letting people know he was a proud boy from Winnsboro, Texas.

T. C.'s grandfather came to America in about the early 1800s from England. Isaac Martin Chadick began a slow migration to Texas with his family that began in Virginia, then to Tennessee and Alabama. They arrived in Texas in 1845, settling two or three miles west of present day Hughes Springs. Walter Martin Chadick, father of T. C., was born in Camp County in 1864, and 1892 he married Carrie Ozella Mars. Walter and Carrie first moved a mile north of Winnsboro, then acquired the 125-acre Alvis place in the northeast part of town, where he farmed sixty of those acres.

Martin and Carrie Chadick had six children: Clifton, Ethel, Herschel, Era Mae, Jack, and T. C., the youngest. T. C. attended school at Winnsboro, graduating with honors from the new high school on South Main Street. He excelled in all sports, and after high school he attended SMU in Dallas on a football scholarship. When he overheard the freshman coach ask his name at the end of the season, T. C. realized his SMU football career was limited. After giving it much thought, T. C. transferred to Burleson Junior College at Greenville.

Law was T. C.'s second career choice. While at Burleson, he often visited the Hunt County Courthouse and listened as interesting cases were being tried. In 1932, during the midst of the Great Depression, T. C. decided to pursue a legal career. With encouragement from local attorneys and family financial support, he enrolled at Cumberland University. He graduated from the Cumberland School of Law in 1933, passed the Texas bar, and began a law practice in Winnsboro.

T. C.'s legal and political career began as a city attorney for Winnsboro. He was also a county attorney for Wood County, and served as a state senator from Tyler from 1941 to 1949. During those years, his private practice was in the areas of the state, tax, probate, oil, gas, and land matters. He was appointed District Judge of Wood and Upshur Counties in 1949, and, in 1956, he was elected to Chief Justice of the Court of Civil Appeals. T. C. served on that court until his appointment to the Supreme Court of Texas in 1977. He retired in 1979, but continued to hear cases and write opinions as a senior judge until 1999.

Judge Chadick established the Chadick Family Scholarship Fund in 2002 in appreciation of his family and the people in the community who made it possible for him to attend college. I have been honored to serve as a member of the Chadick Family Scholarship Fund since its inception in 2002. Scholarships of up to $3000 are awarded each year to Winnsboro students, and it has benefited a variety of students in their quest for higher education. Judge Chadick told me once that this was his payback to the good people of Winnsboro.

In 1985, T. C. gave the ground for the Gilbreath Memorial Library in memory of the Walter Chadick family.

I grew up with the Chadick family as neighbors, and all I can say is that they were good folks, and good neighbors who always offered a helping hand. My dad said many times, "Your role model should be a man like T. C. Chadick."

## Vocational Agriculture

Since Winnsboro is in such a rural farming area, it is important to note the impact of the vocational agriculture classes in Winnsboro schools. Those classes have played such an important role in developing a strong agriculture base for Winnsboro and this section of Wood, Franklin, and Hopkins Counties. Two Ag teachers who have been instrumental in developing and efficient program for the last forty-eight years are Burke Bullock (1964 to 1994) and Richard Lovern (1988 to 2012). Both were catalysts for the WHS Ag Department, but the program began many years prior.

The Winnsboro chapter of the Future Farmers of America had its beginning during the height of the Great Depression in 1934. At that time, a row-crop farmer was fortunate to have a mule and a piece of land to farm. Many were sharecroppers, and farm prices were so low that sometimes farmers could not even recoup the cost of their seed money. A good cow might bring fifteen or twenty dollars.

It was in those conditions that the FFA chapter had its beginning, under the supervision of C. T. Simms. The classroom was located in the basement of the 1925 high school on South Main Street, across from the present City Hall. The Ag Department did not have a shop, but male students were taught the rudiments of agriculture. They were given instruction on tree planting and grafting, methods to improve the soil, how to handle erosion, how to run terraces, construction, and other farming chores. Their contributions to the community included working cattle and hogs, de-horning cattle for stockmen, and culling laying hens.

Each student had a project, like tending an acre of watermelon or corn, feeding out calves and hogs, or any other project related to agriculture. Part of the curriculum of the class involved keeping records on what the project cost, time involved, and the gain or loss on the project. This is where many local businessmen got their start.

In 1942, Lester Cole came to Winnsboro as the Ag teacher. Under his leadership, members of the FFA chapter at the school involved themselves in several projects and sponsored an ongoing citywide campaign to keep the community clean. Another project involved a cooking facility where people could bring fresh meats and vegetables to be canned. During World War II, that kind of processing became necessary as so many items were rationed.

Several years, and several Ag teachers later, R. E. Johnson came to Winnsboro from Mount Pleasant in

1945. He remained as the head of vocational agriculture for thirty-four years, until his retirement in 1979. The FFA chapter experienced rapid growth during that time and received state recognition.

In 1950, Bill Pollard joined the program as a second Ag teacher. The classroom moved from the basement of the high school into a two-room building west of the school, and a much needed shop was added. FFA students constructed a broiler house where the present high school is located today. Every year, barbecued chicken would be served at the father/son banquet and profits from the chickens were used to help defray the cost of the chapter's summer trips.

Winnsboro FFA began to spread its wings as one of the state's outstanding agricultural programs for leadership and training under Johnson and Pollard. Joe Dan Boyd, a strong leader, was elected president of the Texas FFA in 1952 and later earned the American Farmer Degree, the highest award attainable in FFA. Tommy Boyd was elected president of FFA Area VI in the 1953/54 school year.

A community pavilion was built at City Park in 1984, with money derived from the Hay Show. In 1997, the FFA chapter assumed sponsorship of the Hay Show. According to figures passed to me, the Hay Show has benefited Winnsboro FFA in the amount of around $800,000.

In the 1980s and 1990s, local Ag students were showing broilers at the Houston livestock show and rodeo, as well as calves and steers at the State Fair of Texas in Dallas and the Fort Worth livestock show.

In 1992, the livestock judging team won first place at the Houston livestock show judging contest. The dairy team placed second in competition at a big event in 1989 at Texas A&M University.

While I was a student at Winnsboro high school, I was part of the FFA chapter. I remember one year, when our project involved feeding out two calves until they reached seven hundred to seven hundred fifty pounds, we announced a Friday 10:00 a.m. sale for the calves and waited at the Ag barn for two hours, but not one buyer came to the sale. Finally, the calves were led to the sale barn on Farm to Market Road 852, where the livestock sale had just begun. They cleared the ring for the calves, and the Winnsboro Livestock Commission gave us five cents above top market price. We were happy with the outcome.

Whenever I go to the Hay Show, or some other FFA event, it makes me proud of this community, and my thoughts returned that day many years ago, when disappointed Ag boys had a calf sale and no one came.

**The following article is taken from the Winnsboro Tribune Wednesday, June 26, 1996**

Today, let us climb aboard one of Mr. Henry Ford's Model T automobiles and cruise down memory lane to Winnsboro High School in May 1921, just before graduation. We are here to do a story about the senior class for the Peckerwood Flat Gazette.

The high school building is located about where Memorial Middle School cafeteria is situated today. Several large oak trees surround the campus. The high school was completed in 1911, with the first graduating

**Reflections of Winnsboro**

class in 1912. The south part of the campus serves as the football field and basketball is played on outside court behind the school.

As we go chugging along this bright spring morning, we come to a halt in front of the school and out comes a smiling young lady named Helen Alvis. She is the associate editor of the high school annual staff, and she greets us with a warm welcome to Winnsboro High School. We ask Helen what all the singing is about upstairs, and she replies, "Oh there's an assembly program in the study hall, and the glee club is performing for the student body."

We pause for a moment to listen to the students as they sing "Look for the Silver Lining" and "Wait Till the Sun Shines, Nellie."

The high school annual is called The Alberta, after the peach that grows in abundance throughout this part of East Texas. This year's edition is dedicated to professor M. A. "Dad" Westbrook, the brilliant science teacher, who has gained the respect and affection of the students for his devotion to education.

The pictures of six teachers are on the faculty page of the high school yearbook. The first is J. H. Sheppeard, who is completing his twelfth year as superintendent. He also teaches math. English and Latin are taught by Miss Hymon, and Miss Holley teaches home economics. As mentioned, Dad Westbrook teaches science, and Miss Collins teaches history and English. Mr. Hargis, the principal, also serves as a teacher and coach.

Now we take a look at the section of the yearbook reserved for senior class pictures. There are twenty-two scholarly-looking young ladies and gentlemen dressed in their Sunday best for the picture. It appears they are just itching to finish high school and meet the exciting world of the Twenties Century. A few of the well-known seniors of that class are Fred Azbell, Russell Cannaday, Willie Campbell, Helen Alvis, Alice Winkle, and Lulu Gilbreath.

The first social of that school year was a hayride to Musgrove Springs, where a delicious picnic dinner was served. Next, that class had a Coke party at Fowler's Drugs and a night trip to a sugarcane patch. Other activities for that senior class included a Halloween party at the home of Bess Connor, several trips to the Amusu theater, candy-making parties, and costume and bunko parties. During a slumber party, the senior girls all went down to the train depot to watch the 12:45 a.m. special arrive, serenading the passengers as the train came in. Who could ever forget the party at Mr. Sheppeard's home, when he played the fiddle as Mrs. Sheppeard served a delicious meal; or the party at Eugene Gibson's home, where the girls were allowed to draw a slip of paper for a stroll with some eminent young gentleman?

The senior class of 1921 began its education on September 1, 1909, at the Winnsboro school on Pine Street, which is now the school administration building. On that first day of school, a group of timid little boys and girls, clinging to the hands of their mothers, entered the first-grade room at the school and were greeted by their teacher, Miss Ada Brock. Soon, those leaders of the future were focused on reading, writing, and arithmetic.

**Reflections of Winnsboro**

Before long, the class of '21 entered high school as young men and women, saying goodbye to the North School and accepting the added challenge of high school. At first, it was difficult for some of the boys to wear shoes in warm weather, but before long most came to school in long trousers and spent more time combing their hair than studying. During freshman year, the girls became a little more proper and the boys began to take an interest in athletics.

As tenth grade rolled around, that was the time most of the boys and girls caught a disease known as puppy love. Then all at once the first-graders of 1909 were high school seniors. The time had come to share words of wisdom with the freshmen and sophomores, reflect on the past, and get ready to meet the future.

After this look at the class of 1921, we close the yearbook, thank Helen for the tour, and extend congratulations to the happy seniors of the 1921 (end of 1996 article).

## Chapter Eight – Prominent Men & Businesses

The Cannaday family moved to Winnsboro from Purley in 1879. Mr. Henry Cannaday told the story that he and his brothers cut trees from the streets around Memorial Middle School, which was then known as the Lawrence property. They were given the wood as payment.

In September of 1907, H. L. Cannaday Dry Goods opened its doors at 215 Main Street in the building which previously had been occupied by mercantile businessmen, John and Patrick. When the store first opened, Winnsboro was a small village with mud-filled streets and plank sidewalks. It was impossible to keep mud tracks from littering the floors in stores, and open doors offered the only relief from the heat during the summer months; running water and electric lights were luxuries of the future. Kerosene lamps furnished light, and water wells furnished drinking water. Wood stoves provided heat in the winter.

The new H. L. Cannaday business formed a partnership with Winnsboro that would last many years. In 1925, Russell joined his father in the family business after graduating from Baylor University. The Cannaday family built a reputation on honesty and integrity. They offered good clothing at reasonable prices. If a customer did not have money and needed credit, Mr. Henry, or Russell, usually extended a little help to purchase what was needed. Cannaday Dry

Goods offered anything from a pair of work shoes to Sunday slippers, or a pair of overalls to a nice dress.

Many farmers bought their brogan work shoes at Cannaday's, and in the early days, work shoes cost four dollars or less. Mr. Henry and Russell would invite customers to come by on Saturday for a visit, and they would put neat's-foot oil on work shoes free of charge. That proved to be a pretty good public relations gimmick, because the store stayed in business for sixty-six years.

As a young man, Dr. Henry Frank Cannaday worked at the family business for his father Russell. Henry has vivid memories of Winnsboro in the late 1940s and 1950s, including the colorful drugstore philosophers who sat on the curb, as well as details of the town's history passed on to him by his father and grandfather.

## R. H. McCrary

Hardee "R. H." McCrary was involved in about everything that happened around Winnsboro for over fifty years. He was born on October 5, 1882, to Tom and Dema Gray McCrary near the Coke community. In 1907, McCrary married Vinnie Edwards in Pleasant Grove and started farming, but he soon realized that a farming career was not what he was looking for in life. He opened a grocery store at Coke, but by 1912, he relocated to the booming town of Winnsboro and went into the grocery business at 207 North Main Street. Tiring of a slow grocery business, McCrary moved down to Smoky Row and opened a furniture/hardware store. Then around 1920, he moved back to Main Street and opened a furniture/hardware business in the Robertson building, which is now the First National Bank parking lot.

In 1929, McCrary bought out Bob Wilkinson's hardware and funeral parlor at 216 North Main, as well as buying a house and lot from Wilkinson on West Elm Street. McCrary immediately demolished the wood-frame house and replaced it with one of Winnsboro's most fashionable brick homes.

The upper floor of the building on Main Street was used for storing caskets and the embalming equipment, with the hardware store operating on the lower floor. McCrary Mutual Insurance Company was established in about the early 1930s.

McCrary was a longtime public servant and town leader. He served as director of Farmers Cotton Oil Company, director of First National Bank, and was a deacon at First Baptist Church. He served two terms as mayor of Winnsboro, and was a member of the city council and the local school board. He was actively involved in highway planning and development, agriculture projects, water conservation, and oil development. In 1958, the Winnsboro Chamber of Commerce named him Man of the Year, and in 1968, he was selected by the East Texas Chamber of Commerce as Man of the Month. In 1971, then in his eighty-ninth year, R. H. McCrary was honored as the oldest native-born citizen of Wood County by the Old Settlers.

R. H. McCrary set a precedent for customer service while he was an active businessman. He always treated customers the same, whether the purchase was for ten cents' worth of nails or if they were buying an expensive bedroom suite. He would be found sitting behind his desk posting in a ledger, but always stood to extend kind wishes to customers and ask if he could help them. In the old days, a plow point, churn, harness, or a wagon could be acquired at McCrary's for a reasonable price. He was a friend to everyone, especially farmers. If something could not be found at any other place in town, it could usually be located at McCrary's hardware store. In 1973, R. H. McCrary passed away and was laid to rest beside his devoted wife of fifty-five years at Lee Cemetery.

## Charlie Robinson

Charlie Robinson came to Winnsboro from Wylie in about 1915 as an aggressive young man intent on becoming a successful entrepreneur. When he arrived, Wood County did not have a cleaning/pressing business. There were only tailor shops to spot-clean clothing, brush items, and hand press clothing. Charlie found a location in the first block of East Elm Street and installed a steam boiler and water lines. After acquiring cleaning and pressing equipment from Dallas, he put up a sign which read, "Open for Business." His doors remained open for more than fifty-five years. After adding a clothing line, he advertised "Chas Robinson Good Clothing."

Robinson and his wife, Trudie, had one daughter, Valla Faye, who was a dignified English teacher and taught at Winnsboro High School for more than forty years. Once, while in Miss Robinson's class, sitting on the back row with my head resting on the desk, she walked to the rear of the room and tapped my resting head with her pencil and requested that I answer a question. My reply, "I don't know the answer."

She said, "You've had time to dream the answer."

After that embarrassment, I never rested my head on the desk during class again. Though Miss Robinson was a disciplinarian, she displayed a sense of humor that day.

Mr. Robinson had a good line of quality clothing, and a Botany 500 suit sold for fifty dollars, ten dollars under market price. Before my high school graduation ceremony at the Rock Gym, Joe Grady Tibbs and I visited Charlie Robinson's clothing for graduation suits. Each of us was fitted in a nice double-breasted suit, then we both chose two-tone brown and white shoes, which were popular at that time. We told Mr. Robinson we only had money for the suits and shoes, but we each needed shirts, ties, belts, and socks to match.

Charlie never lost a sale. He said, "I'll give each of you a shirt and tie to match the suits, but that's all—I'd lose money on the sale."

We told him Perkins Brothers had a cheaper Curlee suit on sale and began to leave. He said, "Wait a minute. Being as both of you are graduating and are good customers, I'll throw in the belts and socks to match the suits."

When we picked up the suits, they had been pressed and had a nice handkerchief placed in the pocket of each suit coat. Later he would kid me about "putting it to him."

Some years later, when I was teaching school in El Paso, a package arrived from Chas Robinson Good Clothing Winnsboro, Texas. When I opened the box, I saw it contained a beautiful pair of alligator shoes. I had often told Mr. Robinson that I would love to have a pair of alligator shoes, but could not afford a $140 pair of shoes on a yearly salary of $3,800. He enclosed a note, which read, "Just pay me when you have the money. Shoe salesman gave me a deal on the shoes at $95. Your friend, Charlie."

He remained a friend throughout life.

## R. G. Andrews

R. G. Andrews might be described as "The Shaker" of Winnsboro for twenty-eight years. He knew how to make things happen with his manner, attitude, and confidence. In the city's early years, Mr. Andrews would ride to town each morning in a shiny carriage pulled by two matched horses driven by a coachman dressed in a black suit. When the vehicle stopped at the front entrance of the Andrews Emporium, the coachman placed a step at the carriage exit for Andrews to step down, then handed him his gold-knobbed cane. This seemed to be the lifestyle portrayed by the "merchant prince" of Winnsboro.

In 1896, business mogul R. G. Andrews, who was not yet thirty years old, built the Andrews Building at the northeast corner of Main and Broadway. The impressive building, which covered four lots, was one of the largest and finest two-story business establishments between Dallas and Shreveport. Mr. Andrews, known as a dealer in just about everything, bragged about stocking anything a person needed from the cradle to the grave.

This was no idle boast, for besides carrying dry goods, he had a grocery store, hardware store, furniture, harness and saddlery shop, building materials, window glass, paints, buggies and wagons, motor vehicles, and even an undertaking parlor. In 1901, R. G. Andrews built another two-story brick structure, this one extending from Main to Market Streets. Andrews had the builder construct a second-story crosswalk above the alley connecting the two buildings, providing easy access from one building to the other.

Once, Andrews entered Charlie Morris's office at First National Bank and requested a loan of a few thousand dollars. Morris turned him down, saying he had overextended his credit. Andrews smiled and graciously departed. The next day, he caught the train to St. Louis. Two days later he returned to Winnsboro with a check for $200,000 from a St. Louis financial institution. Andrews then went to Charlie Morris's bank and, with a big smile, requested that Morris personally handle the deposit of the check into Andrews' account. Both men were strong Winnsboro business rivals.

## Banks and bankers

Thomas Shelton and Will Pearson are remembered as the town's first bankers. Both were pioneer business merchants, and before an official bank was ever established in Winnsboro, any merchant who had a little money to loan and a safe in which to secure assets might be called a banker. They would hold customers' cotton and timber proceeds in their vault for safekeeping without a charge. Over the years, Tom Shelton would own the four-different unincorporated private financial institutions in Winnsboro and serve as the president of two national banks, one in Winnsboro and the other in Texarkana.

It was while in the hardware business that Mr. Shelton began offering loans to farmers who needed a little cash to make a crop. He carried a small ledger book in his coat pocket, containing the names of customers, the amount of the loan, interest charged, and their account balances. If you were behind on your loan payment, Mr. Shelton would go to your home, find you out in the field, or stop you on the street, and proceed to discuss your business loan. He must have been persistent, because several old-timers related the following to me about Mr. Shelton, "There were three things you had to do in early Winnsboro—pay your taxes, pay uncle Tom Shelton, and meet your maker."

Tom Shelton first operated a private bank in Winnsboro during the late 1890s, then in 1901 he joined C. B. Gorman and others who organized the Farmer's National Bank, which began operation in January 1902. The bank was originally located in the 1901 R. E. Skeen building, then moved three doors south on Main Street in 1903. In 1905, Shelton sold the Farmer's National Bank to Manton Jones and moved to Texarkana, where he became president of the City National Bank of Texarkana.

Banking in this area of East Texas started in 1892 when the Morris family formed the Camp County Bank at Pittsburg. They immediately became interested in business prospects for Winnsboro, and in January 1893, S. S. Morris and sons Charles H. and R. A. (Lon) arrived in Winnsboro to establish a bank. The outlook was good, with a thousand citizens without banking facilities, and several local merchants purchased stock in the new business. The group, headed by the Morris family, acquired a building at the southeast corner of Main and Elm Streets.

On March 10, 1893, the M&P bank, a private financial institution with $15,000 capital, opened for business. It was the opinion of many that the bank would close within six months. Townspeople wanted to be sure their money would be safe. Some folks had the idea that the bank would charge for taking care of their money, while others thought the bank would fold and their money would be lost. In 1895, S. S. Morris turned the Camp County Bank over to his son Lon and the Winnsboro M&P Bank to his son Charles. On January 1, 1901, the M&P bank was nationalized and became the First National Bank of Winnsboro. In 1907, First National Bank acquired the assets of the Farmer's National Bank, leaving the city with one bank.

One story that Mr. Morris enjoyed telling about early days of banking in Winnsboro went something like this: One day a man entered the bank and asked to borrow twenty dollars. He wanted to know what it would cost him for sixty days. Mr. Morris approved the loan, but wanted to make the loan secure. The man said he understood and agreed to the proposed terms. When the note was made out and handed to the new customer for his signature, he signed the instrument then took a twenty-dollar bill from his pocket and handed it to Mr. Morris, who pinned it to the note. Banking was something new to Winnsboro. In spite of early problems, the M&P Bank, with the support of stockholders as encouragement, grew.

The bank showed a steady profit and growth during its infant years. By 1905, the bank had amassed assets of more than $300,000. It soon became known as the "Old Reliable" bank of Winnsboro.

On January 22, 2016, the First National Bank of Winnsboro received the prestigious Texas Treasure Business Award from the Texas historical commission.

## Doctors

Dr. Titus S. Skeen came to East Texas from Georgia after the Civil War and practiced medicine in his home. A well-respected man in Winnsboro, Dr. Skeen constructed the town's first medical clinic. Dr. Skeen was born in 1843 and died in 1919.

Dr. C. E. Eskridge had a home on North Main Street where he practiced medicine; he was the first doctor in Winnsboro to perform abdominal surgery. After Dr. Eskridge died, his wife, Anna, married M. D. Carlock Sr. and she was the mother of M. D. Carlock Jr. Dr. Eskridge was born in 1863 and died in 1905 at the age of forty-two.

There were two Baber brothers, both medical doctors, and both had hospitals in Winnsboro that were built by Will Gorman. The W. L. "Will" Baber sanitarium, as it was called then, was located at South Main and Myrtle Streets, while the George Baber Sanitarium was on the corner of North Main and Sage. Both men were born in Cherokee County, Georgia, and each was considered an outstanding medical doctor.

Will Baber graduated from Southern Medical University in Atlanta in 1894, at the age of twenty-one, and he did postgraduate work at John Hopkins University in Baltimore, Maryland. Later, during his work at the University of Chicago, Dr. Baber made discoveries as to the anatomical structure of the human body and the science of medicine accepted by leading authorities. In 1908, he discovered the effect of quinine on the malarial parasite. Dr. Will, a renowned surgeon, practiced medicine and performed most surgical procedures in Winnsboro for more than seventeen years. Often, he was called for consultations in Dallas, Chicago, and Baltimore about surgical procedures. He never neglected his patients or turned anyone away because of their inability to pay. Dr. Will had the energy and drive to work long hours, but the thing that curtailed his outstanding research into new surgical techniques was his failing eyesight.

In 1914, Dr. Will bought the two-story house at 306 South Main Street from local lumber baron Hardee Russell. The house became the Baber Sanitarium. Patients came from all areas of East Texas seeking his medical advice, and his practice kept him busy eighteen hours a day.

My friend, the late M. D. Carlock, told me that as a young boy he would walk up South Main past the Baber hospital around nine-thirty in the morning and see Dr. Baber performing surgery on the screened-in front porch, where the morning light shown the brightest.

By 1918, Dr. Will needed additional space for his medical practice, and that's when he had Will Gorman build the two-story brick structure on West Myrtle.

**Reflections of Winnsboro**

That modern equipment medical facility would serve Winnsboro until 1921.

By November of that year, Dr. Will's vision had failed and kidney problems became a constant companion. He was admitted to St. Paul Hospital in Dallas, and, at the age of forty-nine while in the prime of life, this country doctor from Winnsboro died. The Baber Sanitarium was left to Dr. Baber's daughter, Mrs. Birdie Mae Speights, a long-time respected Winnsboro schoolteacher who used it as her residence. It had become an apartment house much later when it burned.

Some of the prominent doctors of the 1930s and 1940s were Dr. Ross Mathis; Dr. Stevenson, a dentist; Dr. Louis Hightower; Dr. Earl Stuart, who served as an Army doctor in WWII; and Dr. Frank Wheeler. Dr. Hightower, father of Louis "Red" Hightower, had his offices on the Bowery in a two-story building.

Dr. Wheeler, father of long-time Winnsboro resident Becky Wheeler Pickett, opened his practice in about 1936, after serving as an army doctor. He was known to be a compassionate doctor, willing to put off a night on the town with his family if there was an accident and people needed help. His other daughter, Karen Wheeler Pendergast, went to Austin, and later came back to Winnsboro with her husband, Tom Pendergast, who purchased The Winnsboro News. Dr. Wheeler's son, Burt Wheeler, was an avid football fan, and was always hanging around the Red Raider Football field. He liked to take care of the players, and was eventually put on staff as the equipment manager.

I remember Dr. Wheeler as a good man who took me under his wing, talking to me often about right and wrong.

## Winnsboro newspapers

The first newspaper in Winnsboro was established by R. L. Hayes in about 1878. He had recently arrived in the area and determined that the community of approximately three to four hundred people could support a weekly newspaper. He established The Sentinel in one of the small shanties near the railroad depot. Hayes was also one of the organizers of the Texas Press Association, and he attended the Second Annual Convention, which was held at Pillot's Opera House in Houston.

In the late 1880s, F. M. Sewell moved to Winnsboro and purchased assets of the paper, changing the name to The Messenger. That newspaper operated here until 1898, then Mr. Sewell moved to Wolfe city.

Another newspaper, the Winnsboro Wide-Awake, was established in 1891 by Tom Napier. According to records, F. M. Sewell was one of the investors in the new publication, so he must have returned to Winnsboro by then.

By 1905, the paper developed financial problems and publication was suspended.

The Winnsboro Free Press was established by Jake Rhodes in 1893, and there are inaccurate records of other small publications springing up. The clearest link to the present-day newspaper is from 1905 when the Winnsboro printing company was organized. The officers were R. G. Andrews as president, T. G.

Carlock as vice president, and R. M. Smith as secretary. If this was the beginning of The Winnsboro News, it was only published from 1905 to 1908, then it merged with The Messenger and became The Winnsboro Weekly News.

Homer Weir, thought to be a native of Pittsburg, acquired The Weekly News in 1909 and operated offices on East Elm Street. In 1910, The Wide-Awake was acquired by The Weekly News, and in 1912, The Weekly News and The Free Press shared office space in the Rhone building on West Elm Street. A fire in 1914 destroyed most records of both newspapers. Assets of The Free Press were purchased by Weir, and it became part of The Winnsboro Weekly News. Homer Weir published the paper until 1927. That's when he was killed by an automobile while crossing the street at Main and Elm. Mae Weir, his wife, continued publishing the paper until 1943, and retired after thirty-five years. Gray Ford Jones acquired The Winnsboro Weekly News in 1943 from Mae Weir, and in 1951, he changed the name to The Winnsboro News. In 1985, Tom and Karen Wheeler Pendergast purchased the newspaper and published it until Tom died in 2013. Karen died in 2009.

Bill Jones and Mary Naney McMillan, granddaughter of Nancy Cook and great-granddaughter of W.R. McMillan, placing the first historical marker in Winnsboro in 1984. (Courtesy of Bill Jones)

William Rile McMillan (R) and John Elliot Winn were the two men who paused at a crossroads of two trails in what was to become Winnsboro, and decided it was a fine place to live. (Courtesy of Bill Jones

Nancy Cook, who convinced the East Line & Red River Railroad to come through Winnsboro, and not Webster, and was responsible for establishing the early community, and the RR depot in 1876. (Courtesy of Bill Jones)

John McMillan, son of William McMillan, who became a prominent Winnsboro citizen and civic leader. (Courtesy of Bill Jones)

The McMillan home built in 1885. (Courtesy of Bill Jones)

This is Winnsboro's first city hall, which also housed the Chamber of Commerce and the Fire Department. Winnsboro had two fire trucks in the early 1920s. Firemen of that era wore white shirts and bow ties. (Courtesy of The Winnsboro News)

This is the Baber Sanitarium, the name given to Dr. George Baber's hospital, that operated in Winnsboro until the early 1960s. (Courtesy of the Winnsboro News)

Dr. Will Baber, brother of George Baber, had his clinic on West Myrtle Street. Often consulting with Johns Hopkins and the University of Chicago, he was one of the most well-known medical doctors to come from Winnsboro. (Courtesy of The Winnsboro News)

Dr. C. E. Eskridge had a home on Main Street where he practiced medicine until he died at a young age. (Courtesy of The Winnsboro News)

Dr. Robert T. Dickey was a well-respected physician in Winnsboro in the early 1930s. He was killed in a car accident in 1936. (Courtesy of The Winnsboro News)

Dr. Frank Wheeler, father of Becky Wheeler Pickett, Karen Sue Wheeler Pendergast and Burt Wheeler, practiced medicine in Winnsboro after a stint as an Army Doctor in World War II until he died in 1965. (Courtesy of Becky Wheeler Pickett)

Chalybeate Springs Hotel was known as a resort and spa in the 1880s, and when the hotel closed in 1895, it became the home of Gus Garrison, a prominent Winnsboro citizen and civic leader. The Masonic Lodge in Winnsboro was named for Garrison. (Courtesy of The Winnsboro News)

The annual Autumn Trails Festival that is held in Winnsboro every October was started in 1957 with a trail ride. It grew over the years to add other weekend events such as the Swap Meet and the Arts & Craft Fair, as well as the Antique Car Rally. No matter what weekend folks attend, they are sure to have a good time.   (Courtesy of The Winnsboro News)

The Autumn Trails Festival started with an idea that maybe trail riders would like to come to Winnsboro for a weekend in October when the trees were adorned with beautiful Autumn colors. Many came, and many continue to come. (Courtesy of The Winnsboro News)

The parade to kick off the Trail Ride weekend of Autumn Trails goes through downtown Winnsboro every year. It has always been a great draw, with lots of folks coming to welcome the wagons and the riders. (Courtesy of The Winnsboro News)

The Antique Car Rally was added to the Autumn Trails activities and Bob Willis made quite a statement with his Model T that he adorned with old washtubs and milk cans. "Autumn Trails or Bust" has been part of the car parade since the early 1960s. (Courtesy of The Winnsboro News)

South Ward School was built in 1911 as Winnsboro's first high school. (Courtesy of The Winnsboro News)

Some of the Black children in Winnsboro attended the Dunbar School, which was built by the Rosenwald Fund in 1927. It was one of three schools serving the Black community. (Courtesy of Earnestine Starling)

Earnestine Starling was one of the teachers who influenced the lives of several generations of Dunbar Students. She was once a student there, as was Fannie Mae Wright, another outstanding Dunbar teacher. (Courtesy of Earnestine Starling)

The Winnsboro High School band. (Courtesy of The Winnsboro News)

The Lady Raiders basketball team. They won a tournament championship in 1934, and the winning tradition continues to this day. (Courtesy of The Winnsboro News)

The old Rock Gym, restored and renewed.
(Courtesy of Bob Williams)

An early home of The Winnsboro News, which started in 1905 and continues to publish a weekly paper today. (Courtesy of The Winnsboro News)

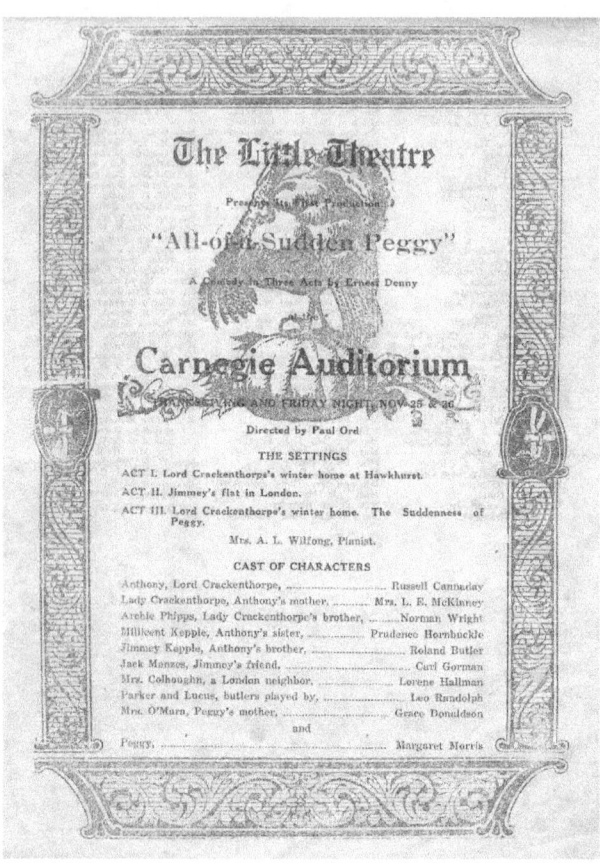

The Little Theatre Playbill – The first theatre production, "All of a Sudden Peggy", held at Carnegie Auditorium, featuring local players, Russell Cannaday, Mrs. L.E. Mc Kinney, Norman Wright, Prudence Hornbuckle, Rolant Butler, Carl Gorman, Lorene Hallman, Leo Randolph, Grace Donaldson, and Margaret Morris. Directed by Paul Ord.
(Courtesy of The Winnsboro News)

The corner drugstore where young people like to hang out in the 1930s, '40s and '50s. (Courtesy of The Winnsboro News)

Seated: L-R: M.D. Carlock Sr., Lucy Dickey, wife of Dr. Dickey, unidentified.
Standing: L-R: Mrs. Alf Morris (Craigie) and Dr. Eskridge. They all were prominent Winnsboro residents in the early 1900s, active in civic and community events. (Courtesy Bill Jones)

The Old Rock Gas Station on Elm Street that is believed to be the last place Bonnie & Clyde stopped on their way out of Winnsboro on that fateful day they were killed in Louisiana. (Courtesy of Bob Williams)

A busy day on Main Street as farmers brought produce to ship on the railroad. (Courtesy of Bill Jones)

## Chapter Nine – Outlaws & Other Criminals

Perhaps the most notorious visitors to Winnsboro were the infamous Bonnie Parker and Clyde Barrow, who often made a stop in Winnsboro when traveling from Dallas to hideouts in Louisiana. Since Winnsboro is located at about a halfway point, it was always a good place for the couple to stop and get provisions and perhaps some rest before heading east.

Much has been written and filmed about Bonnie and Clyde and their exploits, and unfortunately much of that has been sensationalized and isn't all historically accurate.

When I lived and worked in Dallas, I had the occasion to meet a man, Frank King, who had grown up in Dallas and went to school with Bonnie Parker. Frank took me around West Dallas and pointed out the poor neighborhood where she was raised and the school he and Bonnie attended. Then we drove by the deserted service station and garage of Henry and Cumie Barrow, parents of Clyde. I remember it as mostly a sheet-metal building with two gas pumps.

Frank's memory of Bonnie was as a smart and likable classmate, a cute girl of small stature. Most all the kids from this school came from a poor economic background, but Bonnie seem to be a bright spot, looking for a chance to better herself. The day that we visited the neighborhood, Frank looked at the old school building and talked about Bonnie's demise with sadness in his voice.

Bonnie's father died when she was four, and her mother, Emma, moved the family from Rowena to Cement City near Eagle Ford in 1914. Young Bonnie managed to finish high school and worked as a waitress. She was an honor student in high school and excelled in creative writing. She won a County League contest in literary arts, and even gave introductory speeches for local politicians. Described as intelligent yet strong-willed, she was an attractive young woman.

While in school, she seemed to be intent on making something of her life, but she made a bad decision when she married Roy Thornton at age sixteen. They lived together for a brief period before he ended up at Eastham Prison for bank robbery. The marriage was short-lived. They separated, but never divorced. She was still wearing Thornton's wedding ring when she died.

My friend James Cash has visited with me on several occasions, sharing stories of Bonnie and Clyde. James said he gave Ralph Fults a job at Chance Vought Aircraft in 1956, not knowing at the time that he had been a member of the Barrow Gang. Later, after Fults told James the whole story, it was the beginning of a life-long friendship. On March 18, 1993, Ralph Fults, the last survivor of the Barrow Gang, died at the age of eighty-two.

According to one story that Ralph told James Cash, Bonnie had said that the picture of her smoking a cigar was only a humorous act while she was joking around with Clyde. She said she never smoked cigars and resented the press making her appear as a gun moll, smoking cigars. Ralph told

James that members of the Barrow Gang avoided Bonnie for fear that Clyde would kill them if they appeared too friendly.

The most credible story of Bonnie and Clyde's first meeting was that it happened in January 1930, at a mutual friend's house in West Dallas. Bonnie was out of work and was assisting the girlfriend, who had a broken arm. Clyde dropped by while Bonnie was in the kitchen making hot chocolate. They did not meet, as legend has it, while she served as a waitress at Hargraves Café.

Around 1970, I became acquainted with a man named Ted Hinton. He lived in Irving, and at one time had owned a motel and later a restaurant. When I met him, he was an older man who enjoyed coming to a local coffee shop for conversation with friends. I would often listen to the interesting tales those men told, not realizing that the stories were pages of history. In 1932, Hinton had become a Dallas County Deputy Sheriff at the age of twenty-seven. Sheriff "Smoot" Schmidt assigned him to assist Texas Ranger Frank Hammer and "Manny" Gault in a shoot-to-kill order against Bonnie and Clyde.

Ted had been acquainted with a young Bonnie while she worked in Marco's Café as a waitress. Because of her looks, male customers would flirt with her. Mr. Hinton, always a gentleman, treated Bonnie with respect. He admitted that he had a crush on Bonnie, which made it difficult for him as one of the men sent to kill her and her lover, Clyde.

Once, during a conversation with the morning coffee bunch, someone mentioned my East Texas connection to Winnsboro. Hinton spoke up and said that he had been to Winnsboro on several occasions while serving as a law enforcement officer. At that time, I didn't understand the significance of the statement, but later I found historical data indicating that a posse was waiting for Bonnie and Clyde at Winnsboro close to the time they were killed.

When I first read the story *Bonnie and Clyde*, written by Bonnie's mother and Clyde's sister, my thoughts for a moment were that she wasn't so bad, only misled by Clyde. The paperback book described Bonnie as a poor little girl growing up in West Dallas without financial means, who received love and understanding from her family, never caused problems with the law, but could not dig herself out of the hole of poverty living in West Dallas.

Then I remembered the people she hurt and those who lost their lives.

Soon after meeting Bonnie in 1930, Clyde was jailed for burglary in Waco. He escaped using a handgun smuggled past the guards by Bonnie, but was caught a week later in Ohio and sentenced to fourteen years in the Texas penitentiary.

Clyde was put to work picking cotton with another person, Ralph Fults, who advised him on how to survive, and immediately a friendship developed. In August 1931, Ralph was paroled and in January 1932, he helped Raymond Hamilton break out of the McKinney Jail. In January 1932, Clyde received parole after purposely having a fellow inmate cut off two of his toes so he could no longer work.

Immediately, Bonnie, Clyde, Ralph Fultz, and Raymond Hamilton formed the Barrow Gang. This time has been described by historians as the real beginning of their crime episodes. In April 1932, the gang attempted a burglary at Mabank. Barrow and Hamilton escaped on two stolen mules, but Bonnie and Fultz were captured. The outlaws were placed in a small one-room jail with a dirt floor. Bonnie was released after telling authorities that she had no part in the fight and was only an innocent victim. She was using the name Betty Thornton.

Bonnie and Clyde were not smart or efficient thieves. They never made plans, but constantly moved around. When they ran out of money, they would rob a bank, grocery store, or gas station, often risking their lives for twenty or fifty dollars. Two thousand dollars represented a huge haul. Clyde fancied himself as a modern Jesse James, and avoided killing innocent victims and mostly shot law enforcement officers.

On August 5, 1932, Barrow and his associates were drinking alcohol at a Stringtown, Oklahoma dance. This was during Prohibition where alcohol was not permitted. Deputy Eugene Moore attempted to arrest the outlaws, but Clyde killed him. This is the first recorded killing of a lawman by the Barrow gang, only the first of nine officers of the law who would eventually be slain. After killing his first victims, Clyde had blood on his hands, and he knew the road only led to mortality for him and Bonnie. There would be no turning back for either of them.

The outlaws continued to run, all the while committing crimes. On March 22, 1933, Clyde's brother, Buck, and his wife, Blanche, joined the gang, along with W. D. Jones. They were all hiding out in Joplin, Missouri in a garage apartment. Lawmen suspected them of being bootleggers and attempted to make an arrest. Clyde and W. D. Jones killed one lawman and wounded another. When they ran, the gang left everything behind, including a camera with an exposed roll of film. The Joplin Globe developed the film which contained now-famous photos. It had the photo of Bonnie in a moment of joking, posed with the cigar in her mouth, which she detested.

The desperate characters of lawless acts stayed on the run and constantly moved from one place to another. On July 24, 1933, after bungling a robbery attempt at Platte City, Missouri, the gang was in Dexter, Iowa, driving two cars. Local lawmen discovered their whereabouts, and there was a shoot-out. Clyde, Bonnie, and W. D. escaped on foot, and Buck was shot in the back. Blanche was hit in the face and eyes by flying glass and was arrested. Buck died five days later and Blanche received a ten-year prison term.

By January 1934, Clyde was back in Texas and made his move against the Texas Department of Corrections in the infamous escape of Henry Methvin and Raymond Hamilton at the Eastham Prison. During the escape and shootout, Maj. Joe Crowson was killed. Then the Texas Department of Corrections contacted former Texas Ranger Frank Hammer and convinced him to accept a commission as a Texas Highway Patrol Officer and to serve in the prison system as a special investigator, specifically to hunt down Bonnie and Clyde and the Barrow Gang.

On April 1, 1934, Clyde had parked on a lonely road at Southlake, Texas. Two Motorcycle Highway Patrolman approached the car, thinking there was a problem with the vehicle. The other passengers were Bonnie and Henry Methvin. Henry fired shots into both officers, and Barrow fired at one officer. Methvin is believed to be the killer of patrolman H. D. Murphy and Edward Wheeler. Before the shooting started, Bonnie had been sleeping in the back seat. Methvin, in his confession statement, said she offered to help the dying officers.

## Bonnie and Clyde often visited Winnsboro

During the time that they left a trail of crime across the Southwest, the Barrow Gang often returned to the confines of East Texas, driving a stolen Ford V-8, which would outrun police vehicles when souped up. Clyde, a good mechanic who had a masterful understanding of engines, sent a letter to Ford Motor Company praising their "dandy car."

Clyde's first gangster car in 1932 was a Model A Ford. When they traveled as a gang, they always drove two cars, with Parker and Barrow in one, and the other gang members in the other. According to folklore, the outlaws often visited Winnsboro for two to three days. Then they would show up at Carthage, Center, and Nacogdoches where Clyde had relatives.

Jack Nichols, a small-time Dallas hoodlum, became acquainted with the gang and would provide a sanctuary near Pleasant Grove. For a price, he obtained food, ammunition, and firearms. Jack was raised in Pleasant Grove and knew places of concealment. As a man from Pleasant Grove once told me, "We always knew when the outlaws were here because they hid their car in the Nichols' barn with the barn doors closed. Otherwise the doors were always open."

Members of the Barrow Gang were never known to have committed a crime in Winnsboro. Why law enforcement officers in Winnsboro never attempted to arrest them is a mystery. The couple quietly came into town, drove up and down the street several times, then stopped to eat at John Grimm's Grocery and Café. Clyde always entered the café first, ate a bowl of red-eye chili or a hamburger, while Bonnie waited in the car, watching the road and observing movement of pedestrians up and down the street. Afterward, Bonnie would eat while Clyde kept watch.

Some stories indicated that Winnsboro might have been called Bonnie and Clyde's "safe haven" because the lawman didn't bother them, and they had friends here. Undoubtedly, the authorities had the attitude that if the couple didn't break the law, they wouldn't bother them. Even so, people were fearful of the gang. Every time a Ford V-8 fitting the description passed at a rapid speed, folks thought it had to be Bonnie and Clyde.

Dewitt McElyea was raised near the Crossroads Community, and before he died he related the story to me that happened in 1933. Dewitt said that one hot summer morning he went to the thicket behind the Hopewell Baptist Church, looking for their milk cow that had gotten out during the night. He saw an automobile parked in the trail. As he approached, a man and a woman quickly emerged from the vehicle with pistols in their hands. They were wild-looking, faces welted with mosquito bites, and they were dirty from sleeping in the woods. McElyea inquired about the cow, and the couple said they had not seen it. McElyea quickly departed, knowing that he had stood face-to-face with the outlaws Bonnie and Clyde.

Deloy Wilson from Pleasant Grove had stories of Bonnie and Clyde passed on to him from his parents. According to those tales, Bonnie and Clyde often slept in the Hopewell Church and had a fire pit in the woods south of the church, outlined with rocks, where they prepared meals. Once, someone found a woman's watch around the cooking area with the name Bonnie Parker inscribed on the case.

J. T. Mullinax sat down with me several years ago, and we discussed what is thought to be Bonnie and Clyde's last visit to Winnsboro. Early one morning in May 1934, a '34 Ford V-8, tan in color, with Louisiana license plates, stopped in front of Dickens Beauty Shop at the southeast corner of Elm and Market Streets. At that time, East Elm Street was a part of State Highway 11. J. T.'s aunt, Mertie Dickens, served as a hairdresser. In walked Bonnie Parker, who asked to have her hair fixed. Mrs. Dickens said Bonnie had an injury where a bullet had grazed her skull. She went ahead and did the best she could while Bonnie gazed at the street. When Mrs. Dickens finished, Bonnie looked in the mirror and offered a nice compliment. All the while Clyde, remained in the vehicle with the engine running most of the time, watching every car that passed on the street.

Gail Bain and I often talk about a story concerning her grandfather and his exploits with Bonnie and Clyde. In 1933, Bradley Willis received an appointment as a special ranger by Governor Miriam Ferguson. Willis was near Tenaha-Timpson, on an unpaved road and approached another vehicle that was stuck in a water crossing. Other occupants of Willis's Model T were his wife and four sons: Tom, John, Robert, and Arthur. Bradley walked up to the automobile where a man and woman were standing and inquired if he might offer help. The nervous couple thanked him, and then Willis recognized the outlaws but chose not to challenge the couple in a gun battle because of the danger to his family. After Willis helped to dislodge the Model A, Clyde walked back to the Willis car and gave Robert a quarter while making friendly remarks. Willis's weapon was in the front seat covered by a pillow. Mr. Willis always said Bonnie never took her flashing eyes from him during the entire time.

## The end is coming

By the beginning of May 1934, Bonnie and Clyde were scared and on the run, as law enforcement agencies from across the Southwest were moving in from all directions. Like wounded animals, they were attempting to escape, but few avenues remained open to them.

The word across Texas by the Highway Patrol was to get Barrow, especially after the way the two highway patrolmen were gunned down west of Grapevine.

John Paul Cofer, a retired Department of Public Safety officer, gave an account of how the Highway Patrol stationed in Texarkana in May of 1934 worked hunting the killers. The Texas Highway Patrol set up roadblocks at crossings of the Red River, eight miles north of Texarkana, at Fulton, twenty miles to the northeast at Garland, and twenty-two miles east of Texarkana. Officers manned the roadblocks for several days, sometimes remaining on duty for over twenty-four hours.

The blockade was called off on May 20, 1934.

The notorious gang managed to elude all law enforcement, and Bonnie and Clyde continued to stop in Winnsboro when they were nearby. Legend has it that they never robbed or killed anybody in Winnsboro, and most of the stories I've heard seem to bear that out. Bonnie would go to the beauty shop, and she would also go to a local store to buy clothing. Mrs. Knight relayed a story about the first time the Bonnie came into the store, "I waited on her. She seemed to be in a hurry and I could only fit her in a Junior size clothing. She left in a huff, but about two weeks later appeared once again." This time Mrs. Knight had clothes that would fit Bonnie, and afterwards every time the outlaws were in town, Bonnie would come to the store and buy clothing. Mrs. Knight said that Bonnie would often offer to hug her. Mrs. Knight said, "She reminded me of a lost little girl, not a wanted criminal."

# Reflections of Winnsboro

# The final chapter

On May 14 or 15, 1934, Jack Nichols was driving a stolen vehicle drove from Dallas to Winnsboro early in the morning. He stopped near the front of the railroad depot, where he met Bonnie and Clyde to deliver guns and ammunition. Jack was supposed to receive one hundred dollars for the delivery, but Clyde stalled and asked him to return the following Tuesday night for the money. Nichols, although mad, reluctantly agreed.

Nichols left Winnsboro and ended up at the Gladewater Tourist Court, where he had a few drinks and where lawmen discovered the hot automobile. Nichols was arrested and placed in jail. While being questioned, he admitted to eleven criminal charges and he admitted going to Winnsboro to deliver guns and ammunition to the Barrow gang. Then he offered to lead a posse there the following Tuesday.

Meanwhile, the Barrow Gang remained in Winnsboro and had breakfast at Dean's Café on 205 Main Street. After eating, Bonnie went up the street to either Cannaday's or Dodgen's to pick up a sack containing clothing. Clyde waited on the sidewalk, observing cars and pedestrians.

After Bonnie got the clothes, the outlaws left in their vehicle, driving up Main Street to East Elm. They stopped at the Rock Station on East Elm for fuel, and then headed down State Highway 11 toward Pittsburg. This was their final visit to Winnsboro.

Bonnie Clyde and Henry Methvin then took an alternate route over desolate country roads from Dangerfield to Atlanta, Texas, and then to a hiding place known as the "pick up" location in Louisiana, where they remained for the next two to three days.

Meanwhile, a posse comprised of Frank Hammer, B. M. "Manny" Gault, Ted Hinton, and Bob Alcorn had set up an ambush in Winnsboro. After three days of waiting, news was received that the outlaws had been spotted at a Shreveport café. On May 21, 1934, the four lawmen immediately shifted their surveillance to Louisiana.

In a final effort to escape law enforcement, Bonnie and Clyde headed from Shreveport to Gibsland, Louisiana. At two o'clock on a Wednesday morning, May 23, 1934, Ted Hinton, Deputy Bob Alcorn, former Texas Ranger Manny Gault, Texas Ranger Capt. Frank Hammer, retired, Sheriff Henderson Jordan, and Deputy Prentice Oakley of Louisiana gathered in the woods eight miles from Gibsland and waited on the top of a hill that offered a long view of the road.

They waited until after 9:00 a.m., and then thought the outlaws had returned to Texas. Then the roar of a light tan 1934 Ford V-8, heading south at a rapid rate of speed, could be heard as it approached the hill. When the car came to within forty to fifty feet of the officers, the firing began. The posse, under Hammer's direct orders, did not call out a warning. It was all over in a matter of seconds. Clyde's head flew back and Bonnie toppled forward. The car careened to the left and ran into a sandbank.

## Reflections of Winnsboro

Posse members had fired one hundred thirty rounds. They emptied their automatic rifles as well as shotguns and pistols toward the car. Following the ambush, officers inspected the vehicle and discovered an arsenal of weapons, including stolen automatic rifles, semi-automatic shotguns, handguns, and several thousand rounds of ammunition along with fifteen different license plates from various states.

While researching the life of Bonnie Parker, I found her to be a hotheaded spitfire and a thief but did not discover evidence of her actually killing any of the victims credited to the Barrow Gang. When Frank Hammer was asked why he killed a woman who was not wanted for any capital offenses, he answered, "I hated to bust the cap on a woman, especially since she was sitting down. However, if it wouldn't have been her, it would have been us."

Clyde is buried in the Western Heights Cemetery and Bonnie in the Crown Hill Memorial Park, both in Dallas, near their childhood homes. The following from one of Bonnie's poems is inscribed on her grave marker: "As the flowers are all made sweeter by the sunshine in the dew so this old world is made brighter by the lives of folks like you."

The tale of Bonnie and Clyde is mostly an accumulation of stories passed to me over many years. It's intended to be factual, but some of the accounts represent folklore from the prior generation. It is my opinion that a lot of the truth involving Bonnie and Clyde will never be known; the reader must decide which is fact and which is fiction.

## "History is lies agreed on"

Throughout my life, several tales have been passed on to me about May 23, 1894, when it was said that the Dalton Gang robbed the First National Bank of Longview, then fled to the territory of Oklahoma, passing east of Winnsboro while escaping.

Well, in my opinion, it didn't happen the way some folks and press related the story. As Mark Twain once elaborated, "History is lies agreed on."

I would not go that far, but when the story has been passed along for more than one hundred years, it sometimes ends up differently from when it began. I have done some research in an attempt to record the event as accurately as possible.

On that May morning in 1894, the sleepy little town of Longview was getting ready for a normal day of business. It was a late spring day with activity around the blacksmith and harness shops. Children played in the streets and the buzzing of the saw at the lumber mill broke the silence. Saloons were open for business, and ladies were shopping for lace and spools of thread at the Mercantile.

North of the town square, the First National Bank had its usual business, with merchants and farmers coming in to pay mortgages or make deposits. Nothing unusual at this East Texas farming community that pleasant morning.

Four riders on horseback stopped near the bank entrance. They were led by the man thought to be Bill Dalton. Other members of the outlaw gang were Jim Jones and his brother Bill, and George Bennett. Bill

## Reflections of Winnsboro

Dalton and Jim Jones entered the bank and announced it was being robbed. Bill Jones and George Bennett were stationed outside in the alley to observe any actions by citizens. Suddenly, a bank customer ran from the bank screaming, "The bank is being robbed!"

Pedestrians on the street scurried to find cover and merchants grabbed their weapons. From an alley position, Bill Jones began a rapid fire, and a man in the street suffered a fatal wound. Another man who was standing on the courthouse steps was killed, and several others were wounded. The outlaw George Bennett was shot and killed near the alley by a hardware merchant.

The remaining three outlaws took two hostages as shields and made their getaway. With guns drawn they fired up to forty rounds in each direction with a posse in pursuit, but they were not apprehended. Eventually they released the hostages without injury. It has been said the outlaws got away with between $200 and $2600 of bank money.

Bill Dalton, along with the injured Jim Jones and Bill Jones, probably had a place to lay low for the next two days because they seemed to disappear. Then they attempted to reach the territory of Oklahoma with the posse in pursuit. Their trail of escape led near Newsome, and the telegraph reported the bandits were headed west near Winnsboro.

### Reward makes them targets from rowdy citizens

A dozen Winnsboro men gathered at the local saloon and formed a posse to apprehend the outlaw gang. The hefty reward of an undetermined amount served as an incentive to the men to pursue the so-called Dalton gang. After a number of belts of the hundred-proof snake oil, some posse members inquired about the number of outlaws and how well those outlaws could shoot.

After another shot or two of redeye, the makeshift posse of Winnsboro men left the saloon and headed off to apprehend the gang.

According to stories passed on from Carl Gilbreath, the barber who was acquainted with most of the posse members, the men were saturated with alcohol by the time they left the saloon. Carl said, "They either galloped their horses at a fast pace all the way to Leesburg, or slow-walked their animals so they wouldn't be in Newsome when the outlaws passed."

Carl said the members of the posse were farmers, not gunfighters, and had second thoughts about tangling with a sharpshooting gang. Next morning, the tired and weary posse returned to Winnsboro after suffering a hangover.

For years, they told the story about how they pursued the Dalton gang.

Back then, stories were told of how the outlaws buried a sack of twenty-dollar gold pieces at the Cypress Crossing. Another story said that money was hidden at the Gray Rock Crossing. There is no evidence that any gold coins were ever recovered at those locations, so in my opinion this story must be considered false.

The robbers traveled by way of the Cherokee Trace to near the Red River, then followed a route west to Paris, turning north to cross the river at the Slate Shoals. They were stealing fresh horses along the way. Forty lawmen were guarding the crossings to the east. Keeping west of those men, the gang was successful in making it back home to Ardmore without trouble.

## How accurate is this story?

Some Western historians have said that Bill Dalton never committed the crime and was actually tried and convicted only in the press. There is conjecture that the Dalton gang did not rob the Longview bank; that it was done by another gang.

Several shady characters were killed around Ardmore at that time, thought to be either members of the Dalton Gang, the Doolin Gang, or another gang. George Bennett died on the streets of Longview, Bill Dalton was killed by a posse on June 8, 1894, at his home near Ardmore, and Bill and Jim Jones shot it out with lawmen in West Texas. Jim survived and went on to receive twenty years of jail time, and after being pardoned, died in a saloon fight in Tulsa.

The people who knew the story firsthand have been gone for many years. This account is the way I interpreted the event, but don't start me lying to say it happened just this way. I do know that gold coins were never found at the Cypress Creek Crossing, as some rumors had it, and the Winnsboro posse did not apprehend a single fugitive. The members of the posse only had a bad hangover.

Was Bill Dalton the outlaw who robbed the bank that day in May? We may never know. The evidence to prove it is so thin, it's hard to tell for sure.

## Chapter Ten - Special Places and Events

This article about the City Cemetery was written for the July August September 1994 edition of the newspaper for the Winnsboro Senior Citizen Center. The paper was called The Center Fold.

Winnsboro's City Cemetery is not neglected, but neither is it pristine. The exact date it was first used for burial purposes is unknown. The oldest visible marked grave is that of Andrew Vannoy, who died in 1858, and the first recorded burial is that of a man who was killed at the McGee/Vannoy Sawmill in 1855. The first grave markers used at the cemetery were pieces of sandstone that were placed at the head and foot of the grave. Many of the burial sites have been lost because of neglect. A number of the headstones have shifted and others have been overturned or destroyed by vandals.

Several years ago, the City Cemetery Foundation was re-organized. Its purpose is to provide care, renovation, and historical perspective that would elevate the grounds to a place of pride. Cemetery Foundation member Dewayne Redding donated the Pine Street retainer wall and the sidewalk on Mill Street, and Foundation members raised money, through donations, to place an attractive wrought-iron fence on Mill Street and a chain-link fence on Pine and Blackjack Streets. When public donations are available, the Foundation plans to construct a chain-link fence across the West side of the cemetery, which will completely enclose the property. Other planned projects include renovation of the historical entranceway on Mill and Blackjack Streets, identification of lost burial sites, and repair of broken markers.

Special gratitude is extended to the City of Winnsboro, and City Administrator Jerry Poe, for their dedication to the cemetery. The city provides manpower for maintaining the grounds and offers other valuable assistance. Last October, the first known Memorial Day observance in Winnsboro was held at the cemetery, and another is planned for next October. (end of article)

## Special visitors to Winnsboro

The big news in September 1943 was that a bond drive would be held in Winnsboro. The bond sale did not seem that important the school children. What excited them was who would be coming to town for the event—Wild Bill Elliott, Gabby Hayes, and the beautiful Anne Jeffries, the first singing cowgirl in motion pictures. These Western movie stars were under contract to Republic Studios and were brought to town through the effort of the local State Theater.

People from miles around came to town for the big day on September 30. Barriers were placed across Main Street, and a flatbed trailer in front of the present First National Bank served as the stage. School superintendent E. O. Moore canceled classes for the day so students could attend the show, and the high school band began the entertainment at nine-thirty in the morning. Hundreds of people lined the sidewalks and streets, while others were perched on the roofs of buildings, and by ten o'clock, people were beginning to grow impatient.

Then a shiny Buick automobile drove slowly up Main Street. The band stopped playing as the car came to a halt near the stage and out stepped the man himself, Wild Bill dressed in a cowboy outfit. He waved to the crowd, while the beautiful Anne Jeffries stepped out in her cowgirl costume. Last to emerge was the humorous Gabby Hayes wearing his gun, chaps, and old campaign hat.

Mayor Alf Morris introduced the stars and welcomed them to Winnsboro. He then turned the program over to Toby Wright, who was chairman of the War Activities Committee. With Mr. Wright serving as emcee, the stars entertained the audience for over an hour while selling war bonds in the amount of $75,000. That was a huge sum of money to be raised in a little town that was just emerging from the Depression.

All good things must come to an end, and that was just as true back then as it is today. The idols of the silver screen waved to the crowd and said how much they enjoyed visiting Winnsboro. Then they got back into the waiting car and drove away. Many of the kids stayed and watched until the car was out of sight, just wondering if they would ever see another real-life Hollywood movie star.

## Chalybeate Springs

Chalybeate Springs, also known as Musgrove Springs, was settled in the 1860s by L. M. Musgrove when he opened a health resort. At one time, the community had a post office, hotel, two stores, two churches, and a school. A sawmill and a cotton gin were located nearby. The community is located three miles east of Winnsboro on State Highway 11, and is identified by a Texas historical marker near the village site.

The word "Chalybeate" refers to a people of Asia Minor who were famous for their work with iron, and has no connection to any Native American dialect. It is my opinion that a learned pioneer immigrant named the area Chalybeate Springs because the mineral water is impregnated with iron.

In 1989, Jerry Bolding, the unofficial mayor, compiled a narrative history of the community which served as a basis for a Texas historical marker. Jerry's research indicated that his great-great-grandfather, William Bolding, gave land for the first school in 1881. The Chalybeate Springs School District #10 covered nearly five thousand acres in Wood and Franklin Counties. The school was located five hundred yards southeast of the springs.

By 1922, life in the Musgrove community was about the same as it had been for the past twenty-five years. Nearly everyone was involved in farming and they would have a milk cow, a vegetable garden, and sometimes raise hogs. They tilled the soil using horses and mules, cut their own firewood, made lye soap and ribbon-cane syrup. Women wore bonnets while working outside, especially during the hot summer months, and picnics were a popular outing. To have iced tea during the summer was a special treat because ice could only be obtained by going to the ice plant in Winnsboro or having it delivered. Inside plumbing and electric lights were then unknown, and homes were cold during the winter, with the only heat produced by a fireplace or a wood heater.

Because of so many mosquitoes, malaria was prevalent in the area during the summer months. One of my good friends, the late Helen Beard, said she took her share of quinine and Groves Chill Tonic. She said her ears roared from the medicine, but it stopped the fever, sweat, and chills that accompany malaria.

Roads were practically impossible for automobiles to maneuver in bad weather. Road beds were a quagmire of mud, passable only by horse-drawn vehicles. This is the way it was in 1922 when Walker and Minnie Garrison purchased their first automobile, an open touring car. In 1928, they traded it for a black Hupmobile sedan and this is when Helen learned to drive. She had to sit on a pillow to reach the controls, and her mother would allow her to drive into town for Sunday school and church. Sometime she did not stay for church, but instead would joy ride with friends, whizzing up and down the unpaved roads as a cloud of dust followed the Hupmobile.

During the 1920s, Walker Garrison built operated a sawmill on his Big Woods property near Perryville. This successful operation ended in 1929 with the untimely death of Walker at age fifty-two. Minnie continued to supervise the timber operation, but the Great Depression and unprofitable low prices of timber products resulted in the sale of the mill to B. F. Campbell of Winnsboro.

Helen Beard's great-grandfather, Walker Fore, built a two-story white frame hotel on a hill overlooking the road and valley below. Sometime after the Civil War, Fore married Sarah Davis of Rhonesboro, and their daughter, Sue, married Augustus "Gus" Garrison in 1873. Gus was an attorney, who later became a Methodist minister in the Texas conference. He is most remembered for his outstanding work with the Masons of Texas, and the Winnsboro Masonic Lodge is named after him.

In 1890, Fore was killed when a team of horses ran away from him near Leesburg. Gus and Sue then moved from Sulphur Springs and assumed management of the family estate. They retained business interests in Hopkins County as well, and had one son, Paul.

Twenty-two-year-old Minnie Cowan left her home in Mineola in 1902 to teach school at Chalybeate Springs. Paul Walker Garrison, an eligible bachelor, had been appointed to meet the new lady teacher at the Musgrove depot and escort her in his buggy to the right boardinghouse. She must've captivated him at once, because after delivering her luggage to the door, he tipped his hat and said, "I hope I see more of you."

Two years later, Paul and Minnie were married by his father, who was now a minister at the Methodist Church in Palestine. They had four children: Helen, Francis, Paul, and Harry. Minnie joined the Musgrove Methodist Church, where she taught Sunday school and often swept the church floors. After being married for a few months, Paul and Minnie went to the World's

Fair in St. Louis, returning home to talk about the many wonders of the young twentieth century. One of those wonders was the marvel of electricity, which had not been seen in Texas.

The Musgrove Springs Hotel became the private residence of the Garrison family after the death of Fore in 1890. Helen described her childhood home as a rambling two-story white structure with galleries upstairs and down. The back of the building was U-shaped, with a yard between the wings. Since it had been designed as a hotel, every room had an outside entrance. There were seventeen rooms, two halls, eight galleries with decorative banisters, and four fireplaces.

Helen had vivid memories of the Musgrove Springs Park that had been established by Walker Fore at the bottom of the hill north of the hotel. She said people would come just to drink the mineral water. School picnics were held there, and occasionally a covered wagon would stop and camp overnight. Helen described the place as being enchanting. Drooping willows lined the spring, providing shades for young lovers who came to court or to "spark," as it was called in those days. White violets and purple ageratum grew in profusion, and the spring had a latticed summerhouse over it.

The water, while not distasteful, had a strong smell of iron. "I can almost smell the scents of summer and see it in my mind's eye, with the green grass and the spring gurgling nearby," Helen once said to me.

What a beautiful description of this place that was once a campground used by Native Americans and then served as an encampment for early pioneer immigrants who were searching for dreams in this new land.

## The Rock Gym

As reported in the Winnsboro Area Chamber of Commerce Newsletter, September 2001

In 1920, Winnsboro did not have a gymnasium and basketball was played on a dirt court behind the high school, which is where Memorial Middle School is now today. Practice was difficult during the cold and wet days of winter. In 1927, the Winnsboro high school Cardinals played their games at the City Park Auditorium. By the early 1930s, the third floor of North Ward, which is now where the Administration Building is located, became the basketball home for the Winnsboro High School Woodchucks. Playing there was a challenge as the ceiling was only fourteen feet high, the floor shook, and the bleachers extended into the playing area.

The school trustees and interested citizens realized the need for a gym, but money was not available for such a large sports project. By 1938, the school board persuaded the Work Progress Administration, (WPA) to assist in building a gym for Winnsboro. The WPA was one of the government projects aimed at putting people back to work during and immediately following the Depression.

The land where the Rock Gym was built is said to be part of the John McBride cattle lot. The McBrides

### Reflections of Winnsboro

sold the land and house to Tom Shelton in about 1930, and in 1937, Winnsboro's School Superintendent J. M. McGee bought property from Shelton for $275. McGee then deeded the parcel to Winnsboro Independent School District. The late M. D. Carlock described the lot as a "crawdad pond that held water much of the year."

Construction of the new gymnasium began in January 1939. The sandstone was acquired locally, and the lumber came from area lumber mill companies. Most of the construction workers received a salary of seventy-five cents to a dollar and a quarter for ten to twelve hours of labor each day. They worked for so little because they were just glad to have a job. Work on the building was completed before the end of that year.

The plan was to have Woodchuck Basketball be at the gym in the fall of 1939. This magnificent monument to sports and education impressed the community. We were a poor farming community in the midst of the Great Depression, but we now had a first-class athletic facility with four dressing rooms—all with hot water showers. Many of the athletes, both male and female, had never taken showers with hot water before.

Winnsboro's basketball heroes performed on the hardwood court of this gymnasium from 1939 until the early 1970s. Some of the most famous coaches from Texas were here, and some of the most outstanding athletes from East Texas played here.

In addition to providing a space for the basketball team, the Rock Gym became the fieldhouse for football, a band hall for musical activities, offices for coaches, and an auditorium for concerts. It was also the place where the junior senior prom was held for years. It was in the Rock Gym that many students said their final goodbye to Winnsboro High School. At graduation ceremonies, the school superintendent, the principal, members of the school board, and guest speakers were all seated on the stage as the seniors proudly marched by this last milestone to receive their diplomas.

Beginning April 17, 1941, the school discarded the name Woodchucks for athletic teams and replaced it with the new name, Red Raiders.

As the years passed, some people demanded a new, modern structure. Some referred to the gym as a worn-out barn. This old friend's face began to fade, paint started to peel, and the roof developed leaks. A new gymnasium was constructed in 1974 near the present high school. The old Rock Gym, a monument to the school's past, stood in silence for several years with boarded up windows, and it showed pains of serious neglect.

In 1989, ten former students gathered at the office of former superintendent Jerry Hardy to discuss the idea of saving the gym. After receiving word that two members of the school board favored bulldozing the building and making a parking lot at that location, Mr. Hardy, and most school board members, liked the proposal and agreed to support the project. Jerry told me, "I will back you if you can get a group together to work on this."

Thus, the Rock Gym Preservation Committee was created for the purpose of preserving, restoring, and passing along to the future generations this historic landmark.

The ongoing restorations have been successful through donations by former students, friends of the gym, and beneficial help from the Winnsboro Independent School District. The present superintendent, Mark Bosold, has offered strong support for the gym, saying that tradition plays an important role in our school.

On the last Saturday in October, hundreds of former students from all parts of the country gather at the Rock Gym for the All-School Reunion. It is a time for people to reconnect and enjoy a number of activities throughout the day. The Winnsboro Independent School District and the Rock Gym Preservation Committee sponsor the reunion, which has become an annual tradition.

## Historic Oaklea Mansion

In 2013, the Oaklea Mansion received a very prestigious honor, receiving recognition on the National Register of Historic Places, a register that is maintained by the National Park Service in Washington, D.C.

The 1903, Carlock house, which is now the Oaklea Mansion, was nominated to the register in the area of "architecture at a local area of significance." At that time, there were no other properties in Winnsboro listed on the National Register. The Carlock house was designated as a recorded Texas Historical Landmark in 1966, and it is the fourth historic structure in Wood County to be approved for National Register recognition.

Marcus DeWitt Carlock Sr. was born in Camp County, Arkansas on December 3, 1852. During the Civil War, Carlock followed his father into battle and during combat he was separated from his father, never to see him again. Young Carlock served as a messenger for the Confederate Army and his father, Samuel, died as a prisoner of war after the battle of Fort Donaldson.

In 1865, the Carlock family moved to Pittsburg, Texas. M. D. and his brother, Tom, moved to Winnsboro in about 1880. Carlock studied law and was admitted to the state bar in 1879. He was elected Wood County Precinct Four Justice of the Peace. He served in that post for fourteen years, holding court on the front porch of his grocery store at Broadway and Main Street, where the old City Hall building sits today. He had a successful law practice and owned an interest in several businesses in town. He continued to practice law until his death in 1931. Carlock was a staunch Democrat. He served as State Executive Committeeman for four years and attended many State Democratic Conventions. He was a friend, and strong supporter, of Governor Jim Hogg.

When the United States entered World War I, Carlock offered to raise a company of Calvary, but was turned down due to his age. He served on the Council of National Defense and the Legal Advisory Board.

Upon the death of M. D. Senior in1931, and his wife Anna Lee in 1934, the Carlock home was left to M. D. Carlock Jr. and his half-sister Isabel Carlock Ragley. In 1947, M. D. Junior bought out his sister's share of the ancestral home, and the house became the permanent residence of M. D. and his wife, Rhea.

For more than forty-five years, M. D. and Rhea were civic leaders and active in historic preservation. They were founding members of the Autumn Trails Association. M. D. practiced law for more than forty years and never turned down a client because of inability to pay. M. D. Junior died December 9, 1995. His wife passed away a year later, but not before securing the future of the beloved Carlock home.

Norma Wilkinson and Rhea had become friends, and Norma's husband, Gordon, and M. D. enjoyed each other's company. Rhea asked Norma to buy her home, and Norma indicated she would if it could be turned into a bed and breakfast. Rhea was delighted with the idea, but she did not live long enough to see the finished product. I am sure that my friend, Rhea, died with a smile knowing that Norma, and the many future guests, would love and cherish the place that she had called home for over fifty years.

The 1903 Marcus DeWitt Carlock home, a two-story white structure at 407 South Main Street, sits three blocks south of downtown Winnsboro. The entire home, other than the brick foundation, is constructed of pine and the exterior has always been painted white. The interior has seventeen rooms, with a stunning curly-pine staircase and a wood-burning fireplace in the entry. With only minor changes, the Carlock home retains the same southern splendor envisioned by the original owner. Norma has been very meticulous in maintaining the neoclassical appearance, with its interior contents typical of late Victorian houses.

Throughout the decades, the Oaklea Mansion has welcomed everyone from state and national figures, as well as hosting many parties and many high school proms. Texas governors Jim Hogg and O. B. Colquitt were frequent visitors. Once I invited Congressman Ralph Hall to join me for a visit with M. D. Carlock Jr.. A lifelong Democrat, Mr. Carlock said, "Bill, you know Ralph is a nice fellow even if he is a Republican."

## The corner drugstore

Do you remember when the local drugstore was a place for the youths of the town to hang out? Back in the 1950s, teenagers gathered for conversation or just for a place to spend some time after school. Every stool and table was filled with excited teenagers.

During my "growing up years," Winnsboro had two drug stores on Main Street with fountains and pharmacies. The Rexall Drugstore was at the northeast corner of Main and Elm Streets. Mack and Mamie McWhorter were the proprietors of the corner drugstore, starting in 1923. The employees were Clyde Taylor, who was the fountain manager, Jack Stevens, Jim Jackson, and Reban, the likable custodian.

Adults sometimes complained about the noise made by the kids, but remembering that they had done the same thing not so long ago, they were tolerant. Mr. McWhorter knew how to handle the younger crowd, and the young folks were usually respectful and well-behaved.

## Reflections of Winnsboro

The Rexall had a large magazine display near the front door. Since television had not taken its place in American life at that time, the young people were eager to read the magazines. Boys and girls would come into the drugstore, order a five-cent cherry coke or a five-cent root beer, concocted from ingredients only found at a soda fountain. They would then retire to the magazine stand. Girls enjoyed flipping through the Hollywood magazines about movie stars and romance, while the boys looked at action magazines, sports, and girls in bathing suits. Few purchases were made. At times, there might be five or six kids standing around the magazine display talking while enjoying their favorite beverage.

After about thirty minutes of the noise the teenagers made, Mr. McWhorter would come forward and remind the kids that the magazines were for sale. Based on the exasperated expression on Mr. McWhorter's face, the kids knew that it was time to move on to another hangout. If any of us teens were offended, that feeling would only last until the next day, and then we were back at the McWhorter soda fountain.

The favorite refreshments at the fountain were banana splits, milkshakes, malts, and soft drinks. Kids quickly consumed their beverage, with everyone paying for their own treat, with the exception of those who were there as couples. The boy, who was expected to pay, saved his money and sat with the girl at a table sipping through straws in one drink while gazing into each other's eyes.

Teen romance during the junior/senior years usually didn't last long, and frequent breakups were common. Soon the devastated couple would reappear with different friends, acting like nothing had happened. Since the hurt feelings didn't last long most became friends, not disappointed lovers in this time of adolescent "puppy love" as it was called back then.

The Corley brothers established a drug business here in 1903, then about 1910 the establishment became Fowler Drugs until 1928, when King Cummings became the owner. Cummings Drugs was well-stocked with medicines, notions, and a soda fountain that offered all flavors of ice cream. At one time, Cummings Drugs had two reserved parking spaces near the store entrance that were used for curb service. Customers would park in the reserved spots, toot their horns and a soda jerk would come out to take their order.

King Cummings was killed in the same automobile accident that killed Dr. Robert Dickey in 1936. King's wife, Kate Cummings, managed the store until the early 1940s, when she sold her business to Jake and Willie B. Martin, friendly newcomers who were well-accepted by the community. High school students served as soda jerks at both drugstores. The fountain manager at Martin Drugs was Adrian Crow, always wearing a big smile with something witty to say. Adrian had been a POW of the Germans during much of World War II, but he always remained a personable man despite his horrible experience during the war. The welcoming and friendly atmosphere at the store made it a favorite place for teenagers to sit for a spell.

# Reflections of Winnsboro

In the '30s and early '40s, most local doctors worked out of either the Martin or McWhorter drugstores. Patients would call the druggist to inquire of their doctor's whereabouts. The druggist would contact the doctor, or let the caller know when the doctor would be available to make a house call. The drugstores also provided a room in the rear with a table the doctors could use to examine patients. Folks who came to town from the country would often visit with the doctor at the drugstore examining room. After the doctor's diagnosis, he prescribed medication to be filled by the drugstore pharmacist, then sent the patient home for rest.

In 1968, Sammy Bell moved to Winnsboro and worked for his uncle, Jake Martin, until 1972, when Sammy became the proprietor of the White Drugstore at Main and Elm. When the R. E. Skeen building owned by Russell Cannaday became available in October 1984, Bell purchased the building, renovating the structure and moving his inventory across the street. He served as Winnsboro's downtown pharmacist until Bell's Pharmacy closed in 2012. After forty-four years of running the successful store, Sammy Bell said goodbye to a drugstore lineage that had its beginning around 1900.

Those of my generation spent many hours in the drugstore at the soda fountain, the magazine rack, and in conversation. Today, the corner drugstores have about disappeared. The remaining few are nestled in small communities, patiently waiting for boys and girls from the 1940s and 1950s known as cool cats to reappear with the charm of yesteryear and order a five-cent Coke or maybe a chocolate soda.

## The Masons

Freemasonry came to Mexico from Spain in 1729. The Roman Catholic Church opposed the Masonic fraternity that promoted religious toleration with a liberal philosophy. The Roman Church viewed this as dangerous to their influence and subjected Freemasonry to persecution. In 1738, the Spanish government issued an order against Freemasonry and members of the Lodge in Madrid were arrested as dangerous to religion.

All Madrid Masons spent time in prison, and eight were sent to the gallows. Freemasonry went underground in Spain until 1808, when Joseph Bonaparte assumed the throne of Spain. Joseph Bonaparte was the Grand Master of Masonry in France and he immediately lifted restrictions in Spain.

In Spain and France, Freemasonry differed from that of England and Scotland. In the European mainland masonry was strongly political, while the English masonry discouraged ties to politics.

The United States version of Freemasonry originated in England, then came to the American colonies prior to 1700. Masonic ideas are incorporated into the history of the United States, the Constitution, and the Bill of Rights.

Mexico declared its independence from Spain in 1821. At this time, there was a strong Anglo influx of settlers from the United States coming to this new country known as the Republic of Mexico that included Texas, New Mexico, Arizona, and California.

## Reflections of Winnsboro

The Mexican government looked upon Freemasonry with suspicion, especially Masons coming from the United States. Steven F. Austin worked hard to maintain good relations with Mexico, but when he petitioned to the York Grand Lodge of Mexico for a charter, they never responded. Distrust developed between the government of Mexico and their subjects in Texas, and rigid rules were imposed on immigrants.

In the winter of 1834-35, five Masons resolved to establish a Lodge of Order in Texas. They realized that such an action would put them in danger, as the Mexican government watched over the citizens of Texas with distrust and had spies observing every move. It was known that Freemasonry was barely tolerated by the priests of the Catholic Church, whose influence was all-powerful in Spain and Mexico.

Despite the dangers, Anson Jones, the last President of the Republic of Texas, and four others believed it would be beneficial to form a lodge at a time when people needed fraternal bonds to bind them together, regardless of the consequences. They were dedicated to their effort to establish Freemasonry in Texas.

The meeting place was in the town of Brazoria, in a little grove of wild peach trees. The spot was known as Gen. John Austin's place. It was a secluded location, where the meeting could take place without fear of eavesdroppers. Here, at ten in the morning in March 1836, the first formal meeting of Masonry in Texas was held. It was decided to apply to the Grand Lodge of Louisiana for a grant to form an Open Lodge to be called Holland Lodge in honor of the Most Worshipful Grand Master of that body, J. H. Holland. A petition was drawn up and signed, then forwarded to New Orleans.

Holland Lodge Number 36 was instituted and opened at Brazoria on December 27, 1835. The meeting was held in the second story of the old courthouse. About this same time, problems started with Mexico and soon turned into open hostilities. The Mexican army took over the area where the lodge was located and members scattered in every direction. General Urrea and a detachment of Mexican soldiers took the record books, jewels, and everything else belonging to the lodge.

Most lodge members joined the Texas troops on the Colorado. Anson Jones and his small party secured the Lodge Charter and other papers before joining the little Texas Army at San Jacinto. At the battle of San Jacinto, the Texas Army of 783 citizen-soldiers under the command of Gen. Sam Houston defeated a larger Mexican force of 1,600 under the command of General Santa Anna, President of Mexico. The Republic of Texas had its beginnings as an independent nation on April 21, 1836.

In October 1837, Holland Lodge 36 was reopened in Houston by Jones and a few other Masons. Two other lodges with charters from the Grand Lodge of Louisiana were established—the Milam Lodge at Nacogdoches and the MacFarlane at San Augustine. Delegates from the three lodges met in a convention at the Holland Lodge in the winter of 1837-38, and the three lodges transferred their allegiance from Louisiana. Holland Lodge Number 36 became Holland

Lodge Number One under the Grand Lodge of the Lone Star Republic, later to become the Grand Lodge of Texas.

In 1855, the Masons in Winnsboro received a charter as Masonic Lodge AF&M Number 146, nineteen years after Texas gained its independence. Freemasonry members constructed a two-story Masonic Lodge building in 1857, and were joined by the Masons of Cypress in 1858. Every President of the Republic of Texas professed their loyalty to Freemasonry, beginning with David Burnet, Sam Houston, Mirabeau Lamar, and Anson Jones. Each made a contribution to the advancement of civilization during the early years of Texas. Masonry does not seek publicity, and many people are not aware of their contributions to communities. For instance, most people do not know that Scottish Rite Hospital in Dallas that offers help to crippled children and their families is supported by the Masons. The only requirement to receive help there is that the family is unable to pay for treatment. There are Masonic-sponsored burn centers and eye foundations that offer help to the needy.

The Gus Garrison Lodge Number 1273 was granted a charter in 1937, and it was named in honor of a native of Chalybeate Springs, a community just three miles East of Winnsboro. In 1895, Garrison was the Grand Master of the Grand Lodge of Texas, and led the Masons with a proud legacy. The lodge in Winnsboro has raised thousands of dollars locally to provide help to the needy, especially in providing scholarships to graduating seniors who need financial help.

I extend gratitude to Freemasonry philanthropic endeavors in the United States, and the organization has certainly been a friend to this community.

## The Rotary Club

On February 4, 1905, the first Rotary Club was organized in Chicago. One of the cornerstones of the organization is the mandate that "An organization which is wholly selfish cannot last long. If we as a Rotary Club expect to survive and grow, we must do some things to justify our existence. We must perform a civic service of some kind."

By 1940, the Rotary organization had grown from its infancy and expanded in all directions, and it was on this date that twenty-one Winnsboro citizens gathered in the dining room at McGee's Café, 205 North Main Street, for the purpose of possibly organizing a Rotary Club in Winnsboro. L. D. Lowry and Carl Reynolds of the Mount Vernon chapter explained the services a Rotary Club could render to a community. At the luncheon were five Rotarians from Mount Vernon, five from Sulphur Springs, and three from Pittsburg. The visitors answered questions about the benefits of a Rotary Club. After the presentations, the Winnsboro assemblage voted to organize.

The following twenty-one men became Charter Members of the Winnsboro Rotary Club that day. They were Roland Butler, Gilbert Gibson, Durwood Dodgen, Barney Dodgen, Lloyd Whittle, Mont Waggoner, Dr. Frank Wheeler, Vance Gist, M. D. McWhorter, O. M. Thomas, Charles Bounds, Lloyd Epperson, Earl Stuart, Marcus Patrick, Alf Morris,

## Reflections of Winnsboro

Malvin Cain, Lefty Neyland, O. E. Moore, Ansley Grant, Clyde Raley, and Haskell Beard.

This diverse group of professional citizens offered leadership necessary for growth and development of the town. At one of the first weekly meetings, Rev. C. L. Bounds spoke on the need for an active Boy Scout troop. Malvin Cain appointed a committee, and soon the Winnsboro Rotary Club was sponsoring Boy Scout Troop 392.

During the war years, the club experienced some dark days as many of the local members served in combat during World War II, and all of the Rotarians were involved in some type of patriotic service. After the war, the club experienced better times and by 1948, Rotary really caught fire in Winnsboro. The club went fifty-two weeks with 100 percent attendance, then followed that with a second year of perfect attendance. That set a world record for Rotary International.

People said that Lefty Neyland was the reason for the club's perfect attendance. Lefty was a nice guy—until someone missed a meeting; then he was worse than a nagging wife until the absentee made up for the meeting. Other people say an old goat was responsible for the club's excellent attendance. If a member missed a meeting, he had to care for the goat until someone else missed a meeting. No one knows for sure what happened to the goat, except that David Steed and Clem Krasowski were involved in the disappearance of "Old Billy."

The community of Winnsboro owes much to the Rotary Club for its dedicated commitment. Some of the club's many accomplishments include sponsoring the Boy Scout troop, assisting with the Campfire Girls, supporting Little League baseball, providing band instruments to the high school band, and aiding underprivileged children. They were also responsible for creating the park at Lake Winnsboro, and for nearly seventy-five years supported other worthwhile projects.

Everything did not always work out as expected for the club. In 1949, the float that was going to be in the Christmas parade would not go through the door of the building in which it had been built. Fundraising projects have not always been successful. In fact, during the early '50s it seems so many fundraising projects went bad that the club's treasurer, John Neighbors, remarked in a joking manner that the Rotary could ill afford any more fundraisers.

## First Baptist Church

In the April/May/June 1995 issue of the Winnsboro Senior Citizen News, I wrote about First Baptist Church of Winnsboro. The article was headlined: LIKE A TOWERING OAK THAT CONTINUES TO GROW.

This congregation, organized as the Providence Baptist Church in 1872, changed its name to First Baptist Church in 1880. A small sanctuary that was built in 1880 was replaced by a brick building in 1904. Prominent Baptist theologian the Rev. Dr. George W. Truitt held memorable services here in 1907. An education building was added in 1934, and the 1904 sanctuary was replaced in 1960. First Baptist Church has historically supported local and foreign missions and continues to provide spiritual guidance to the community.

One of the most memorable weekends in the history of the church occurred in March 1995, as the church observed its 123$^{rd}$ anniversary. Several hundred members, as well as former members and friends, attended the activities over the weekend. There was fellowship time in the Fellowship Hall on Saturday, a chance to visit with friends and enjoy gospel music. The church was filled to the rafters for the emotional Sunday morning service, followed by a barbecue lunch at the City Auditorium. At 2:00 p.m., a large crowd gathered near the church entrance. The Wood County Historical Commission presented a Texas Historical Marker to the church at an observance that commemorated the many years of religious commitment to the community.

The Baptist movement in this area had its beginnings in the 1840s, with the arrival of the first settlers. Wood County was formed in 1850 from a part of Van Zandt County, then in 1874, the west part of Titus County became Franklin County. During the first years, Wood County was largely self-sustaining. Most of the early settlers were immigrants from the South who came for the purpose of improving their living conditions and to escape the gathering war clouds in their home states. In general, these people were self-reliant, ambitious, hearty individuals, who came to a new land with hope and faith.

Interest in religion was high among these people, and along this frontier, circuit riders, or wandering preachers, brought the Word of God. It has been estimated that three-fourths of the people in the United States in 1850 belonged to some Christian organization or at least considered themselves Christians.

Churches as we know them today did not exist. Most early religious services were camp meetings, which were held four or five times a year. People would come from far and near; by foot, horseback, and wagon to gather at a designated camp location. This was usually in a pleasant grove of trees that were surrounded by a plentiful supply of water and grass for the animals. These gatherings were for religious as well as social purposes. Sometimes revivals lasted three or four days, but most of the time they began on a Saturday and ended on Sunday afternoon. Folks of all religious denominations were given a chance to dress up, visit with neighbors, exchange news, swap stories, eat good food, and have the opportunity to share religious beliefs. It was a time of courting for the younger set, and it was also a time for prayer, preaching, old-time gospel singing, and rejoicing in the Word of God.

During the Civil War years, 1861 to 1865, most of the able-bodied men above the age of fourteen served in the Confederate Army. Everything came to a halt, and there are few records of religious activities during this period. In 1867 or 1868, Winnsboro Baptists reorganized. Brother T. L. Scruggs, a circuit rider, served as the first pastor for several months before relocating to Mineola, where he helped organize the First Baptist Church of Mineola in 1875.

The Rev. W. H. Gorman became the pastor in February 1873, and served until August 1877. For several years after that, he preached one Sunday each month during the pastorate of others. Brother Gorman

## Reflections of Winnsboro

and his wife offered leadership, which the young church desperately needed during those first years. Mrs. Gorman was instrumental in helping to organize the Ladies Aid Society, which is known today as the Women's Missionary Society. She served as the organization's first president.

In 1879, when the membership was less than fifty, a small church was constructed on the west side of Peach Street near the intersection of Blackjack Street. The sanctuary was completed in 1880 with the aid of a $200 gift from the Winnsboro Education Society. The gift carried the stipulation that the building could be used for educational purposes, and the church building served as the Winnsboro School until 1888, when the Texas Collegiate Institute was built on the hill west of Walker Park.

One of the most remarkable services in the church's history took place on Sunday, January 20, 1907, when the Rev. Dr. George W. Truitt, the great Baptist theologian considered by many to be the Billy Graham of his day, conducted the morning and evening services. When Rev. Dr. Truitt caught the train back to Dallas that memorable Sunday night, the church's huge financial debt had been retired through the gifts of love. Now, the new church building could be dedicated free of debt. Thirty years later, Dr. Truitt reminisced in a letter to First Baptist Church Pastor Roy Johnson that he could still feel the intensity and inspiration of that service. Dr. Truitt said it was one of the most inspiring days that he had ever experienced in all his humble ministry.

## Highway 80

U.S. Highway 80 crosses into Texas at Waskom, and an old concrete marker, shaped like the State of Texas, stands at the entrance. It was erected in 1936. In the early days, Highway 80 crossed the entire country—all 2,671 miles from Savannah, Georgia to San Diego, California. Crossing Texas from the East, travelers would first see large fields of pine trees, beautiful lakes, oil wells, well-kept farms, and small American rustic towns as the highway meandered toward the cities of Dallas-Fort Worth. After passing through the Metroplex, the highway would go on toward the plains of West Texas, where there were more cattle ranches, oil wells, and a glimpse of Western pioneer life.

In the past, motorists on Highway 80 could slow down to watch farmers trudging behind mules while planting or cultivating their crops. In the winter, cotton stalks stood in the fields and smoke trickled from the chimneys of gray shanties.

Across the Deep South and East Texas, Highway 80 now shares the landscape with the newer Interstate 20. Officially, there's no longer any Highway 80 west of Mesquite, but its ghost is still out there in the little towns where it used to go.

The East Texas Tourism Association and other groups have worked to have U.S. Highway 80 designated a Historic Highway, similar to Route 66, which carried travelers from Chicago to Los Angeles. It is an attempt to make the traveler on Highway 80 feel the romance and freedom of old-fashioned American road trip. A waltz across eight hundred miles of beautiful Texas could be as exciting and romantic as it was in 1940s and 1950s.

Travelers could start at Waskom, a small hamlet on the Texas/Louisiana border surrounded by oil fields, pine trees, and abandoned cotton gins. There are several long-time merchants who'd enjoy sharing the local history with visitors.

The next town of significance is Marshall, where the Harrison County Historical Museum is located in the old Ginocchio Hotel beside the train depot. Display cases hold relics of famous Harrison County people: civil rights leader James Farmer; boxer George Forman; TV commentator Bill Moyers; Y.A. Tittle, who played quarterback for the 49ers and Giants; Dallas Cowboys fullback Robert Newhouse; and Capt. Mack Hopkin, a Tuskegee Airman.

Howard Rosser served as Director of the East Texas Tourism Association and was Highway 80's most tireless promoter. In 1958, while Howard was editor of The Winnsboro News, he came up with the idea of an annual autumn festival, and in the fall of 1959, saw the birth of Autumn Trails, which is held every October in Winnsboro.

As Rosser said about Highway 80, "We want to be able to erect signs and publicize what there is to see along the road."

## Memories of traveling on Highway 80

In the summer days of the 1950s, with temperatures that often surpassed the hundred-degree mark in July and August, I remember the smell of automobile emissions and stopping at service stations along Highway 80. While the station man filled the gas tank, washed the windshield, checked the oil, radiator, battery, and tire pressure, the driver watched after getting a cold drink. A big metal container filled with cold drinks sat against the front wall of every gas station. We didn't call them soda water or soft drinks. They were cold drinks, all of them; Coca-Cola, Dr. Pepper, 7-Up, Pepsi-Cola, Royal Crown Cola, NuGrape, Delaware Punch, Big Red, Grapette, and Nehi Orange.

The bottles of drinks were submerged up to their necks in cold water with ice floating in it. You gave the station man a nickel for the drink, fished one out of the water, removed the cap using the bottle opener that was attached to the box, and took a big swallow of the refreshing cold drink. When the vehicle had been made ready to go, you could pay a deposit of three cents for each bottle and take the drink with you to enjoy while driving.

In the later part of the 1950s, a tall electric refrigerated machine replaced the icebox. The price of a cold drink rose to a dime, which was not paid to the station man but to the machine itself.

Many different kinds of signs lined the roadways on Highway 80 from Waskom to El Paso. They have gone the way of the ice wagon, the steam locomotive, and other vanished sights and sounds whose memories have left a permanent sense of nostalgia across America.

There were large and small signs that touted everything from tobacco to automobiles, restaurants, motels, service stations, garages, and where to go for a

### Reflections of Winnsboro

suit of clothes. Some were funny while others were of a serious nature.

The Burma-Shave signs that dotted so many roadways started in 1927 and continued until 1963. Using the jingles worked well as a sales gimmick in the Burma-Shave advertisements. As one drove down the highway, a short message would play out using several signs that were placed about one hundred paces apart. Passengers in the car would look for the signs and shout out the messages. A couple of examples are;

Dim your lights
behind a car
let folks see
how bright
you are
Burma-Shave

Drinking drivers —
nothing worse
they put
the quart
before the hearse
Burma-Shave

## Chapter Eleven – Agriculture: A Way of Life

East Texas has always been agricultural area from the time the first settlers came and planted gardens to raise their own food. One of the most popular vegetables, and easiest to grow, was the sweet potato, and areas close to Winnsboro soon became leading producers.

Sweet potatoes were part of our steady diet in our household while I was growing up. In fact, we sometimes had this vegetable in some form twice each day. At the time, I took a silent oath that once I left home the sweet potato would never be on my plate; however, over the years I have rekindled a taste for this root vegetable.

The sweet potato is a member of the Morning Glory family. It is an enlarged storage root domesticated five thousand years ago and found to be growing in Peru by 750 BC. Native Americans were growing sweet potatoes in abundance in East Texas when the first Europeans arrived.

My wife, Betty, often refers to the sweet potato as one of the healthiest vegetables because of the high levels of vitamin A, C, iron, potassium, and fiber. It is also an excellent source of beta-carotene; one cup of this vegetable contains four times the recommended daily allowance of this nutrient.

Several generations ago, when East Texas pioneer settlers lived on farms, the sweet potato was considered one of the delectable sweets always closely associated with possum, pork, and butter. "Possum and Tates," Pumpkin Yams," and "Great Big Tater in Sandy Land" were phrases familiar to the first immigrants.

Until 1913, sweet potatoes were grown and used only at the home table or to supply local market because there was no curing plant in Texas. Seeing that need, R. L. Cochran erected a small sweet potato curing house in Winnsboro that became the first one in Texas. His process for removing moisture from the vegetable proved successful, and cured potatoes could be transported to markets and preserved almost indefinitely, either in the store or the home. This represented the beginning of a new cash crop for East Texas.

The growing season for sweet potatoes begins in February when seed potatoes are put in hotbeds to grow what are called slips to be transplanted in fields. All sweet potatoes are grown from transplants that are set in the field from April until about July 4. They need moisture to mature. Harvest begins in late July and continues until November. During the winter months, sweet potatoes are stored in specially-built houses where the temperature never goes below the freezing point. They are then washed, sorted, and packed to be shipped to different markets.

In 1917, Pittsburg became the sweet potato center of East Texas. Wort Stewart erected the first curing plant in Pittsburg, known as Pittsburg storage company. The following year, Stewart and H. B. Hoard became active partners. They developed specially-made crates that were identified with labels:

Little Joe, Big Boy, Texas Star, and Honest John. F. E. Prince of Pittsburg manufactured a superior crate that offered a design for more circulation to the potato.

In the early years of the twentieth century, the largest local sweet potato producers, brokers, and shippers were W. A. Nabors, E. R. Crone, and Gilbreath and Cain. During the fall harvest, Winnsboro shipped five thousand bushels of the product each week. Sweet potatoes were grown in fields as small as one to two acres and as large as twenty to twenty-five acres.

The late Truman Gilbreath, whose family grew sweet potatoes in Stout over a century ago, once told me the growing of this root vegetable could be profitable like any other crop if:

"The land had been properly tilled, you had good slips, the right amount of moisture, deer that love to eat the tender plant did not invade your fields, harvest the potatoes at the right time to prevent rot, they were stored in a dry place to keep the moisture low—and your timing was just right in hitting the market. If you did all these things," Mr. Gilbreath told me, "you might take home a few dollars above the cost of planting and cultivating the crop."

In the mid-1930s, tractors had begun to replace the mule for tilling the soil, but it would be several more years before the mule/horse power would disappear. Row-crop farmers might cultivate thirty-five to forty acres in cotton, corn, and peanuts, using mules or horses to pull the plow. It was during that time that truck farming became big business. In addition to sweet potatoes, farmers in the area grew everything from melons, peaches, and strawberries, to peas, beans, Irish potatoes, sweet onions, and squash.

Seventy-five years ago, most local farmers who owned or rented a piece of damp bottomland that held moisture had a patch of either ribbon cane, sugarcane, or sorghum. In the late fall, farmers would cut the cane and haul it to a cane mill, where juice was extracted and cooked into molasses or syrup. Below the mill, would be a cooking area that held a fire box that was constructed from native stone and could be as large as 4' x 10' and extending four feet high.

Some area farmers had their own mills and made syrup, cooking off anywhere from fifteen to four thousand gallons each year. It took from six to nine gallons of juice, depending on the quality of the cane, to make one gallon of syrup.

In 1997, Doyle Taylor took me on a tour north of Pleasant Grove to the farm where his grandfather, Charlie Taylor, lived. The old 1909 prairie-style house still stands as a monument to a bygone era. Back when this house was constructed by Charlie Taylor, country people killed their own hogs for pork, made syrup and lye soap, canned most of their food, bathed in a number three washtub, and washed their clothes in a wash pot. About one hundred yards behind the Taylor homestead is the old syrup mill where Doyle's grandfather made fine syrup.

In the 1920s and 1930s, farm families were larger than they are today. Many of the farmers grew cotton, and the whole family was involved in working the land. After getting home from school, children had chores to do that often lasted until dark, and then on Saturday they had work to do as well. Families struggled during the Depression years when the price of cotton fell, but things improved in later years. However, in the late 1950s, cotton farming in East Texas began to decline and cotton fields became pasture land for grazing cattle.

In 1938, the Winnsboro Livestock Commission offered a local market so ranchers would not have to ship livestock to Fort Worth or some other distant market. Ralph Robinson and Will Rushing were the first owners of the livestock sale barn. The following year, my father, Gardner Jones, who was known as "Gard," and Tunis Coats became owners of the Winnsboro Livestock Commission and owned the company until 1947. Back then, animals sold for fifty to seventy-five cents; an average sale was two hundred head and a big sale was three hundred head. During the early years, stock was sold by the dollar, then in 1943, weight scales were added. It took buyers and sellers a while to get used to the new method.

My brother, J. D. Jones, and Penn Gorman Junior became owners of the local stockyards in 1947 and ran the business for the next thirty-one years. Buyers began coming to the Friday sale on a regular basis and twenty-two employees were required to operate the business on sale days. That boom lasted until the early 1950s, when a drought decimated local herds. It took a while for the livestock industry to recover, but it did experience rapid growth from 1960 to 1980. Farmland that once had white fields of cotton became pastures for livestock, and dirt farmers seem to disappear with the hand of time.

In 1981, R. C. "Shorty" Mitchell and Randy Mitchell became proprietors of the Winnsboro Livestock Commission. They modernized the barn, built new pens, and acquired additional land. Randy continued to operate the sale barn until 2005, when he sold one of Winnsboro's oldest businesses to Shannon Davis of Yantis. In an interview with Shannon he told me, "After attending a livestock sale at the age of five, I knew what I wanted to be when I grew up—a cattle auctioneer. I would practice my numbers by counting as fast as I could over and over."

Shannon and his wife, Tina, named their new business the Winnsboro Livestock & Dairy Auction. It is a USDA-approved facility and continues to update and modernize the way livestock is marketed for producers. By participating in livestock industry conferences and serving as secretary for the Texas Livestock Marketing Association, Shannon is able to stay informed and pass information onto producers. "I want my customers to be successful in the dairy and cattle industry," he says, "and I want agriculture to continue as a way of life for future generations."

East Texas is not normally thought of as cattle country. The cowboy myth about West Texas being ranching country with huge spreads like the XIT and King Ranches, and cattle drives along the Chisholm Trail to Kansas markets, was the nation's idea of Texas cattlemen. However, East Texas is actually where the Texas cattle industry began. The Spaniards introduced cattle to East Texas in about 1690, and by the 1840s, wild cattle roamed the bottom land in the area.

From 1830 to 1845, settlers who were arriving in East Texas found a large supply of Spanish cattle in the bottoms. At that time, most land was not fenced and cattle were there for the taking. These Castilian cattle were later mixed with the English longhorn that came with the arrival of immigrants from England. According to some historians, the Spanish Castilian and the English Longhorns eventually mixed, creating the modern Texas Longhorn. However, this theory is without conclusive proof.

Starting around the mid-1800s, Jefferson served as a major port for shipping beef and hides by riverboat to New Orleans. Jefferson had a meatpacking plant and livestock were slaughtered there for the beef and the hides. Meat was placed in barrels of saltwater to preserve it while in shipment to world markets, and a cow that sold for ten dollars at Jefferson sold for forty-five dollars at New Orleans. Later, with the coming of the railroad, cattle were herded to stock pens adjacent to the tracks for shipment by rail to distant markets.

Some cattlemen drove cattle themselves through the thick woods along the Opelousas Trail to the market in New Orleans. Some of those same cowboys would later participate in the cattle drives from West Texas to the Midwest.

Ranching west of Fort Worth did not become big business until after the Civil War, starting in about 1867. That's when the Indian problems subsided, and the disappearance of the giant herds of buffalo made land available for cattle ranches. The United States Army established a line of forts and other military installations across West Texas, extending from the Red River south to the Rio Grande.

## Reflections of Winnsboro

Before the Civil War, a principal source of wealth in East Texas was raising cattle. Since most of these early settlers were not slaveholders and did not establish large plantations, they were able to concentrate on livestock as well as farming.

Farming has never been an easy way to make a living. Those who are involved in tillage of the soil have always believed in these words, "Farming is the only business in which you go bankrupt each fall, but some way come up with enough money the next spring to buy seed for planting and start all over again."

Needless to say, those whose ancestors arrived in the Winnsboro area a century ago, or longer, trace their lineage back to an agrarian society. The good land has determined cultural habits. Whether we realize it or not, agriculture played a role in all of our lives and shaping our values. In an 1840s speech about agriculture, the U.S. statesman and orator Daniel Webster said: "When the tillage begins, other arts follow. The farmers therefore are the founders of human civilization."

## Chapter Twelve - The War Years

In 1940, the nation had begun to emerge from the Great Depression, but Winnsboro, Texas, as well as the rest of the world, would soon live through a Holocaust that had never been experienced before. But let us first go back to those early years of the 1940s that were a softer, quieter time when it seemed that romance and peace would live forever. It was the time of the Glenn Miller Orchestra, the Sammy Kaye Band, silly valentines, five-cent Cokes, movies, and dancing to the great music of the big band era. It was a beautiful time.

As employment became more plentiful, folks around here once again had a little money and were able to afford a few luxuries. At last, farmhands did not have to pick cotton for thirty-five cents a hundred as they did in 1935. The jobs provided in the early '40s did not pay much, but people could work again and put food on the table for their children. We were coming out of one problem, but another struggle faced Winnsboro and the world, as Poland had been invaded by Hitler's army on September 1, 1939. Then France fell in June 1940. Great Britain was on the verge of capitulation, and the United States attempted to assist her European allies, while building a fighting force at the same time.

This country had a weak military machine after the First World War, having neglected to maintain a strong standing army. Local boys who wanted to join the military were encouraged to join the National Guard.

**Reflections of Winnsboro**

These volunteer patriots were issued uniforms and outdated weapons, then met on the weekend to practice being soldiers. Maneuvers were held at the cotton yard on a vacant land behind the Assembly of God Church. Rifle-range practice was conducted north of town at the Campbell Bottom. This routine continued through the summer of 1940 under the direction of Capt. Tom Mack.

This was not a bad year for farming, as farmers had a market for their crops, however conversation on the street was about the war in Europe and how much longer Great Britain could last after the British lost most of its army at a place in France called Dunkirk. Now, only the Royal Air Force stood between Hitler and London. In the early months of Autumn, Germany controlled all of the European continent.

In November, we began to feel the effects of the war here at home as Company K, the local National Guard unit, was mobilized and shipped out for military training at Camp Bowie in Brownwood, Texas. Parents, wives, and sweethearts said goodbye to their loved ones, not realizing what lay ahead. Most expected the boys to be back home in six months.

In 1941, the talk around town was about the war in Europe, a better economy, a young baseball player named Ted Williams, Sammy Baugh of the Washington Redskins, President Roosevelt's New Deal Policy, and the fifty-six-game hitting streak of Joe DiMaggio.

While people tried to stay focused on what was happening here at home, they couldn't help but keep looking over their shoulder at the dilemma in Europe, never realizing how close these events were to our home fires.

Then it happened.

On December 7, 1941, the Empire of Japan attacked American forces stationed at Pearl Harbor in the territory of Hawaii. President Roosevelt said it was, "a date which will live in infamy" when asking Congress for a Declaration of War against the Axis powers: Japan, Germany, and Italy. It would be nearly four years before the lights would go on again all over the world, and we could once again enjoy the sweet smell of flowers.

By 1943, many of the local men and women were away at military installations. Some fought in North Africa, Sicily, and had taken part in the invasion of Italy. Other servicemen in the Pacific Theater fought at Midway, Guadalcanal, New Guinea, and the Philippines. With many men and women killed in action, or being held in prisoner of war camps, nearly everyone in Winnsboro suffered the loss of a friend or relative. It was common to display a small banner with a gold star in the middle, called a War Service Flag, in the front window of a home to indicate the loss of a loved one.

Men and women who were not serving in the military went to Dallas, Houston, and Port Arthur to work in defense jobs, making airplanes, ships, guns, and tanks. At home, school children were busy collecting scrap iron, cans, newspapers, copper, aluminum, and old tires to be used in the war effort. People were very patriotic, and everyone wanted to do their part.

## Reflections of Winnsboro

President Roosevelt requested that Americans curtail spending and put savings into War Bonds every payday. He urged people to stay calm, but also to be cautious and not share with strangers any discussion of troop movements or any other military matters. A common slogan that appeared in post offices and government buildings was "Loose lips can sink ships."

The year 1945 brought the collapse of the Axis powers, and the unconditional surrender of both Germany and Japan. On May 8, the war in Europe officially came to an end. Japan surrendered on August 14, and the greatest and most horrible war in all of history was at last over. Thirteen million Americans were under arms at the time; 405,399 were killed, 671,278 were wounded.

Thirty-five of those lost in the global conflict had attended school in Winnsboro. In 1947, the Winnsboro Memorial School was dedicated to those former students who made the supreme sacrifice in World War II.

Postwar Winnsboro, 1946 to 1950, saw many positive changes. Returning servicemen needed about everything from credit to buy homes and automobiles to household items and clothing. First National and Cain Banking met the financial needs of the former soldiers, sailors, and airmen. Most were married with young children, and this was the Baby Boomer period. Some of the GIs returned to their old jobs, while others went to work in oil-related jobs. Times were good and jobs were plentiful. Lumber yards and home builders were busy. The first postwar subdivision of importance was the Carol Addition in the northeast part of Winnsboro. Floyd Carroll divided the family farm, which included the CCC camp property, into lots.

The 1940s were a transitional period for the town. We emerged from the Depression, weathered the horror of World War II, and faced the postwar era with new optimism. This was truly a most exciting time in Winnsboro's history.

## Chapter Thirteen - The Oil Boom

In June of 1942, Texas Tea, as oil is called, began to bubble from holes near Winnsboro. Dad Joiner, who brought in the huge East Texas field, had drilled several dry holes around here in 1928 and 1929, but he did not find enough showing to make a producing well as the oil sands were a few hundred feet deeper. It seemed that Columbus Marion "Dad" Joiner was destined to live up to his nickname as a hard luck oil boomer in the early days of oil exploration across the Southwest during the 1920s.

Then on September 3, 1930, an oil well that Dad Joiner sank on the property of Daisy Bradford near Henderson in Rusk County came up gushing. Following that came productive wells near Kilgore and Longview. Gregg and Rusk counties soon became the world's largest oil-producing counties. Another field closer to Winnsboro was discovered at Hawkins in 1940, but still none in Winnsboro. About the only things people in town knew about oil was from a movie that appeared at the State Theatre titled "Boomtown," starring Clark Gable, Spencer Tracy, and Claudette Colbert.

During the summer of 1942, Amerada Oil company sank a test well eight miles west of Winnsboro near the Coke Community. It appeared to be a duster like the others, but at six thousand feet the showing improved, and at 6,320 feet the well gushed in. It was known as the Kennemer #1.

Then by November 1942, twenty-one wells had been completed. The next month, another field came in north of Quitman known as the Goldsmith field. By April 1943, the Tidewater #1 Andy Bacon Discovery well came in as a gusher with 2,100 pounds of pressure. About sixty-five wells initially formed the field. Oil could be produced from six different pay sands. It was one of the world's richest small fields. The Winnsboro and McCrary fields were located south of town.

The Gulf #1 Brewer well, south of Winnsboro, came in a gusher in 1944. Nearly everyone in town went out to see the new-found wealth, and it was an exciting time for the people.

After the discovery of the Wildcat well, Gulf sank another hole, known as the Hornbuckle #1, which produced oil at 9,200 feet in the Rodessa Pool. Next, Gulf hit good pay sand on the J. F. Petty place, and in September 1944, oil tycoon H. L. Hunt personally supervised drilling a well at Webster on the Joe Bailey Craddock farm. In December, Amarada brought in the Gamblin #1.

During the great oil boom, hundreds of people came to Winnsboro from oil towns throughout the United States. Hotels and rooming houses filled overnight. If anyone had a spare bedroom, all they had to do was put up a For Rent sign and name their price. Vacant buildings became hotels. At one time, Winnsboro had three all-night cafes, and the Gulf service station never closed its doors. The White House, McGee, and Pullen cafés were gathering places for the oilfield workers. Often, two hundred or more men would be standing on the sidewalks near the cafés, waiting to go out to a rig, or the café would be full of those returning after working eight hours in the oilfield. This was also the place to be for those seeking employment. If a crew found itself short a man, the driller would pick a man off the street who was eager for a job. The only requirement was that he had to produce a social security number. This is the way many locals went to work in the oil patch.

At that time, the only paved roads were State Highways 11 and 37, with a small section of Elm Street that was paved. Most of the roads in the country were dirt, and usually not wide enough for two cars to pass with safety. Most bridges were constructed from wood, and while they might support the weight of the car, there was no way a heavy oilfield truck could pass. Seemingly overnight, large oil-related trucks appeared, bringing smaller trucks and pipe and other equipment. The parking area next to the train depot resembled an oilfield truck yard. Each day, the railroad brought in oil supplies and equipment. Vacant buildings were leased to oil companies, and banks became company offices. Leases and royalty ownership changed hands daily as "lease hounds" were all over Wood, Franklin, and Hopkins counties attempting to tie up mineral interests. Fortunes were being made by the stroke of a pen, and everyone wanted to get in on the action.

All during the 1930s, farmers did not make enough money to survive on their worn-out farms, now here come oil speculators offering five thousand dollars just to drill a hole and allow the farmers to keep their land. It was a deal too good to pass up, even though the royalty might be worth ten times the amount offered. For many farmers, this was the first chance they had to take the wrinkles out of their stomachs since 1930. Most grabbed the money, paid off what they owed the bank and grocery store, then bought a new car.

Winnsboro was wide open and money was everywhere. We had the usual kind of men and women who follow boomtowns. The manufacturing of illegal alcohol, better known as moonshine whiskey, was practiced throughout this part of East Texas. It has been said that the town had so many bootleggers that they wore badges to keep from selling the spirits to each other. When Saturday night arrived, the rough element represented a problem. The two movie houses, skating rink, and cafes were full, and maybe two hundred loafers were standing on the sidewalks. It reached the point where people were not safe on the streets. Our town marshal, deputy, and night watchman were not a match for the rowdies.

Winnsboro had not been this tough since the saloon era at the turn of the century. The city fathers recognized the problem and went after someone who could contain the unruly element. The selection was a Matt Dillon-type of city marshal named James Spence, better known as "Texas Slim." Slim had been a tough railroad bull around Gladewater and Longview during the Depression years. He was a tall, older man who wore a ten-gallon hat, expensive cowboy boots, and had a large six-shooter strapped to his side.

He was still pretty tough, and the jailhouse in Winnsboro was soon full of drunks, bullies, and other lawbreakers on a Saturday night. Fred Bigham became Slim's deputy, and they made a good team. Fred was the rugged type, who seldom backed down from a fight. People said that if Fred could not whip you with his fist, he would do it with the butt of his gun.

After a while, things in Winnsboro started to settle down, and there was no need for two officers, so the marshal's job was given to Fred Bigham. Texas Slim left town, only to reappear with pictures of Bigham taken while he had been in prison at Huntsville. A big argument took place at Martin's drugstore between Slim and Fred over the pictures, and Fred nearly killed Slim. Friends carried Slim around to Dr. Earl Stewart's clinic and got him patched up, and then Slim rode off into the sunset, never to return.

Fred Bigham served as marshal for a few years, then the city leaders decided the town did not need a two-fisted type of lawman anymore. They gave him his walking papers. Fred, who had made many enemies, should have left town after losing his job, but he decided to remain here for a while. He got into a fight while involved in a game of chance that nearly ended his life. One of our city officials carried him to the Veteran's Hospital in McKinney, where he recovered only after several weeks of medical care. Someone reported that Fred was last running a café in Dallas. He never returned to Winnsboro.

During the oil boom days, around 1943, there was a riot here in Winnsboro on a Saturday afternoon. People were fighting all up and down the streets in downtown. In fact, one man was hung from a sign at the Gulf station. I saw it all happening with my buddy while sitting atop a boxcar that was parked near the Depot. The fighting continued for several hours, and a number of people were injured.

Then, at about five in the afternoon, up pulled a black 1941 Ford sedan that stopped in front of the old City Hall, which is now Prosperity Bank. A medium-sized man wearing a Stetson hat, shined cowboy boots, Western khaki trousers, and a short vest stepped out of the car. Strapped to his sides were two pearl-handled .45s. He was not a big man, looking to weigh probably all of 160 pounds soaking wet.

This was the legendary Texas Ranger Lone Wolf Gonzaullas, whose legend said he killed seventy-five lawbreakers, not including those who may have been killed in fights along the Rio Grande. The lawman stood on the steps of City Hall for a moment, surveying the nearby scene, then he walked over to where the fighting was going on and said, "Boys, it's time to break the scuffle up."

One of the rioters then said something to him, and the Ranger with the darting blue eyes responded, "I will only tell you one time."

As a ten-year-old kid, I was fascinated by all that was going on, and this was my first introduction to that famous Texas Ranger.

After a few minutes, Lone Wolf returned to the City Hall steps and folded his arms across his chest, as his piercing eyes watched the rumbling crowd. Then one by one, the crowd slowly began to disperse. The riot ended, fulfilling the old Texas slogan, "One riot, one Ranger."

About twenty years ago, when I was visiting with Kent Biffle, who wrote the weekly *Texana* column for The Dallas Morning News, he told me another story about Lone Wolf. He said that in the early 1930s, Lone Wolf was stationed at Kilgore, which was then the oil capital of the United States. Conmen, gamblers, pimps, prostitutes, dope pushers, and just about any other kind of unsavory characters from this type of criminal fraternity infested the streets of Kilgore.

During the oil boom era, Kilgore had ten thousand transients, who were residents of a village that could accommodate a population of only about five hundred. The transients lived in tents, wagons, cars, barns, empty buildings, or any space that might be available. They were a rowdy, lawless bunch, and when Lone Wolf arrived, he said it was necessary to slap a few people to let them know who was boss.

Making his rounds on horseback, the Ranger rode in streets deep with mud. On dismounting, he'd traverse rickety wooden sidewalks and go through doors into the tough joints. Crooks balked like mules when Lone Wolf appeared at their door. He battled them all, never backed down or played favorites. Lone Wolf was an honest lawman, the kind of man who never took bribes or any kind of kickback.

When Lone Wolf arrested lawbreakers, he would string them to his trotline. That was a long trace chain attached to the floor of a vacant church building. Men's ankles were padlocked to one end of the chain, and women's ankles were fastened to the other and. The prisoners' restroom was a bucket passed from person to person down the chain.

After a while, a second Texas Ranger, Bob Goss, was ordered to join Lone Wolf at Kilgore. On a given Saturday, Lone Wolf and Goss might have one hundred people on the chain. Lone Wolf said, "We wanted to get the big boys when they hit town before they could get organized and cause problems. Drifters had their choice of three things: Legitimate business. Getting out of town. Or going to jail."

One would expect that Lone Wolf was a hardened, calloused man after a life of chasing lawbreakers, but that was far from the truth. He was intensely religious, active in his church, and a dedicated student of the Bible. He carried copies of the New Testament with him and handed them out to those on the wrong path of life whom he thought might become useful citizen. And he had a soft spot for children.

After a while, thanks largely to Lone Wolf, the town changed. Working men sent for their families. Churches and schools were built. The wooden shanties were replaced with brick buildings and the streets of mud were paved.

While people in Winnsboro did not accept the oilfield folks when they first arrived, the new people turned out to be some of our finest citizens, and many loved Winnsboro so much they retired in the community. If it had not been for them, we might be a ghost town today.

Winnsboro settled down to the slow, easy-going way of life which it had known prior to the discovery of oil. Winnsboro is not a wild city today, but once upon a time in our history we were truly a Texas boomtown.

## Honky Tonks of East Texas – Music and "Spirits"

# Reflections of Winnsboro

After the saloons were closed in Winnsboro in 1910, there were few places to get a drink unless one found a moonshiner, known as the bootlegger. In 1919, the Eighteenth Amendment was adopted, prohibiting the sale and manufacture of intoxicating liquor in the United States and all territories. By 1933, the government finally admitted failure and the Twenty-first Amendment repealed the Eighteenth Amendment.

During the years of Prohibition, it was difficult for people who enjoyed indulging in intoxicating spirits. From the greatest of all Prohibition movies in 1939, titled "The Roaring Twenties," Humphrey Bogart explains why Prohibition wouldn't stop him from making hay in the saloon business. "It's one thing to pass a law and another to make it work," he explains. "There will always be guys wanting a drink."

Prohibition is remembered as an era of gangsters with gats, Eliot Ness and the Untouchables, the Jazz age, speakeasy joints, and the emergence of the FBI. An older farmer once told me of growing corn in 1931 and 1932 when no market existed to sell the grain. He learned the art of making corn whiskey. About once a month, a large Packard would come from a roadhouse in Dallas to pick up the alcohol. He said a three-hundred-gallon tank had been installed in a secure location in the automobile to hold the illegal alcohol where it could not be observed by members of the law enforcement. The farmer was not proud of the story, but he explained, "My children were hungry, and we did not have money to pay bills."

Speakeasy joints and honky-tonks began to appear throughout East Texas in the 1930s. There was one located west of Winfield called the Country Hotel, and two were located north of Mineola on Highway 37. You could always get a drink without much trouble.

When oil became big business in Gregg County in the early '30s, citizens voted in the sale of alcohol. By 1935, Longview, Gladewater, and Kilgore were overrun with clubs of every description. The discovery of oil made Gregg County the richest oil-producing area in the United States; workers had money in their pockets and were looking for entertainment. Most of the clubs were small, with a dance floor, a nickel jukebox, tables, and a bar. People from Winnsboro went to Gregg County for a bottle of whiskey, a bottle of wine, or a case of beer, or to spend some time at a club.

Mattie's Ballroom was located on the Gladewater Road, and it had the reputation as having the best dance music in East Texas. Mattie Castlebury is remembered as an honest saloon keeper who did not put up with the rough crowd. She booked the best talent available and traveling bands were always standing ready to perform at Mattie's Ballroom. Prices were fair and customers felt safe at this club.

The Palm Isle Club, owned by Hugh Cooper, was located on the Kilgore Road near Longview. It opened in 1935 and featured some of the best and most popular musical groups in America. Over the next few years, Cooper provided outstanding performers, including the bands of Glenn Miller, Tommy Dorsey, Jimmy Dorsey, Billy May, Louis Armstrong, and the one and only Ella Fitzgerald. Cooper and his Palm Isle

# Reflections of Winnsboro

Club became a big name across the Southwest, and other small Gregg County club competitors were forced out of business with the exception of Mattie's Ballroom. Most nights it operated as usual with a full house of loyal customers.

At the beginning of World War II, Hugh Cooper received his draft notice. Since he still owed money on the mortgage for the club, he called Mattie Castlebury and worked out a management deal for her to run it during his absence. She took care of it for the two years that Cooper was away, and when he returned, he found that business was booming. Cooper decided to sell the club, and Mattie bought it and closed the ballroom at Kilgore.

Mattie continued to bring top entertainment to Mattie's Palm Isle Club, and it was open Monday through Saturday, charging fifty cents on Friday and Saturday and a dollar when big stars performed.

When her health started to fail, Mattie sold the club in 1951 to Sherman Sparks and Glenn Keeling. They changed the name to the Reo Palm Isle, and business continued to boom. The style of music performed changed from popular to country-western, bringing in a new clientele. The Wednesday Reo Matinee brought in a new breed of performer, some from the Saturday Night Louisiana Hayride, including Johnny Cash, Johnny Horton, Webb Pierce, and others who were on their way to stardom at the Grand Ol' Opry.

A country boy from Mississippi was a Wednesday afternoon fixture at the Reo in 1955. On Wednesday nights, he often performed at a joint east of Gladewater on Highway 80 for fifteen dollars and tips. Then on Saturday night, he would be at the Hayride. He begged Keeling for a chance to sing with the Reo house band—his name was Elvis Presley.

One of the features of the Wednesday afternoon matinee was the opportunity for housewives have a place to dance in the afternoon. They were called pressure-cooker wives because they would prepare a meal in a pressure cooker in the morning and then come to dance. They would always make sure they made it home in time to give their husbands a warm meal when they got home from work.

Keeling sold the club in 1971, and the new owner went after big names like Ray Price, Marty Robbins, George Jones, and Willie Nelson. In the '80s, with the popularity of Gilley's and the movie "Urban Cowboy," it seems everyone fell in love with country music, jeans, and cowboy boots. At the time, the Rio had the distinction of being the biggest honky-tonk in Texas, with performers Garth Brooks, Randy Travis, Ray Price, and the piano playing of Jerry Lee Lewis being featured.

By the year 2000, the bar crowd had begun to change, and most of the old patrons had disappeared. Within a few years, the customer base had dwindled so low that the long history of the Reo came to an end.

## Chapter Fourteen – Sports and Sport Stars

### The Lady Raiders

People in Winnsboro brag about the Red Raider football team, and they also brag about the Lady Raider Basketball Teams that have gone to state championships numerous times. Every time the Lady Raiders went to Austin for the state championship tournaments, they made the town swell with pride, just as the Winnsboro Oilers baseball team was the toast of the town in the 1940s and '50s.

In 1999, the Lady Raiders won their first state basketball championship with a crowd of cheering fans on hand. When the Class III State Championship Trophy was presented, Governor George Bush appeared to congratulate the Lady Raiders, and presented award medals to individual players. Family and friends and supporters of the school athletic program never failed to go to Austin for the games.

A story in an Austin publication said this about the Lady Raider fans, "When Winnsboro comes to town, they bring more fans from the town of three thousand than the big city schools. Fans and students are well disciplined. When they win, everyone is happy, and in defeat, disappointed, but it never shows."

Two of the most ardent Lady Raider fans are Clara Ziegler and Jack Stenner. While in high school, Clara was on the basketball team, and she has been a supporter ever since. She once told me, "In my mind the community as a whole has one purpose: to support 'our girls' completely."

The Lady Raiders went on to win the state championship in 2000 and 2001. With the community behind them, they continue to play hard and make it at least to regional finals.

## Walker Park

Luta Walker, an early Winnsboro music teacher who died in 1918, bequeathed land at the corner of Gibson and Blackjack Streets for Winnsboro's first City Park. Luta Walker specified in her will that the park should be called the McRimmon-Walker Park, as a memorial to her mother, Laura E. McRimmon-Walker.

The park has been enjoyed by thousands of people since the 1920s. Winnsboro high school football was played there until 1939, and baseball, softball, and circus attractions were also held there. It was the home of the Winnsboro Oilers baseball team in the 1940s and '50s, when two thousand or more fans might crowd the park when the Oilers played the Sulphur Springs Eagles.

In the 1930s, during the Great Depression, baseball became summertime's Sunday afternoon entertainment, a time for socializing and visiting with friends. Winnsboro, Pleasant Grove, Stout, Chalybeate Springs, Perryville, Newsome, Pickton, Cartwright, East Point, and other country communities fielded good baseball teams. Some of the notable Winnsboro Oilers players from that era were Babe Bryce, Doyle Taylor, Tom King, John Earl McCrary, and Carl Talbert.

The Oilers were champions of the East Texas Amateur League in 1947, winning over Sulphur Springs in a hot, sometimes spirited contest and what might be called a mini World Series.

In 1949, the Winnsboro Oilers played an exhibition game against the SMU Mustangs, which was one of the premier clubs in college baseball. SMU's baseball team was led by three college football stars: Heisman winner Doak Walker; All-American, Kyle Road; and quarterback Fred Banners, and just about everyone in town turned out for this sporting event. All the bleacher seats were filled and several hundred fans lined the sidelines. Other people watched the game from the hill to the west.

After nine innings, the score was tied at three to three and continued that way for five more innings, until SMU exploded for three runs when Doak Walker hit a two-run single. It looked like the barn door had been shut on the Oilers, but in the bottom of the fourteenth, the team began to rally. An injured Doyle Taylor came off the bench to hammer a two-run single that ended the fourteen-inning marathon that had lasted three hours and forty minutes, and gave the Oilers a seven to six victory over the favored Mustangs. Carl Talbert scored the winning run from second on Taylor's hit.

In 1949, Winnsboro's league record was twenty-five to five, not counting approximately twenty non-league games. More than forty thousand fans attended games at Walker Park that season, and the Oilers won the league crown for the third straight year.

Becky Pickett shared a remembrance with me about the Oilers. As a small child, while living on Mill Street, her mother, Mary Wheeler, would take Becky and her sister, Karen, to the Oiler games. Mary would bring a blanket and spread it along the left-field line next to the blankets of other friends. "We were there for the game, but it became a social event, visiting and rooting for the home team while enjoying popcorn and other refreshments," Becky recalled.

During the Oilers days, Winnsboro was segregated, and space up and down the right-field line was reserved for Black fans. Winnsboro also had a Black baseball team, the Black Cats. One of the notable team members was Sam Kelly, a catcher. If Sam was alive today he would not be playing for a segregated team but would probably be in the major leagues. He was that good.

The Oilers' winning streak declined in the early 1950s, and slowly during that decade, attendance at the games dwindled. That was due in part to the fact that many people were now buying television sets and staying home to watch major league baseball from the comfort of their living rooms.

By the 1970s, Walker Park began to show the aches and pains of old age. The bleachers suffered from neglect and the fences needed major repairs. In 1988, the stands were dismantled except for a few seats, and when it looked like the entire park might fall into ruin, Team Air Express came to the rescue. They were very generous in offering financial aid and other help to restore the park.

## Chapter Fifteen - Things of Note From The 1900s

In the summer of 1902, Winnsboro hosted a retreat for veterans who had worn the gray uniform during the Civil War. Confederate veterans from the Ross Brigade, Ector's Brigade, and the Grandbury Brigade descended on the town of Winnsboro by the thousands.

They did not come with banners waving in the breeze. They did not come in battle dress. They did not march to the sound of marching music, with muskets in hand, but they did come as an army of peace to relate stories with old comrades. Some walked, rode horses, came by buggy wagon, and others arrived by train. Some of these proud men of the 1861 to 1865 engagements wore campaign hats and displayed medals on their blouses to signify their contributions. Records indicate that nearly ten thousand Confederate veterans attended the three-day event that began on a Tuesday. Winnsboro homes were open for the guests. P. L. Hendry made his land west of town available to those who wanted a place to set up camp, and also for headquarters for the various ceremonial activities.

Captain D. M. White of Winnsboro, who had distinguished himself in several engagements, served as the Grand Marshal for the event. The center of operation for the reunion was established at the R. G. Andrews building on Broadway, across from the depot. All ex-confederates registered there, received nametags

## Reflections of Winnsboro

that included the unit in which they had served, a program of activities, and were assigned lodging. They came from many places and were all made to feel at home. The soldiers of the South were met by the Andrews Band, which serenaded the visitors with musical compositions of "Dixie," "The Bonnie Blue Flag," "My Old Kentucky Home," and other old-time melodies that never failed to bring out the well-remembered rebel yell.

The Bonnie Blue Flag, now tattered and worn, was displayed at a prominent location. Bullets and shells had penetrated its folds, but the assemblage cheered with the same energy as they had done in many hard-fought battles. Next to the Stars and Bars floated the Stars & Stripes—the flag of a happy and reunited people. In a sense, it was like the Union soldier was here grasping the hand of the Confederate soldier, and it convinced anyone in attendance that the hallowed past is the heritage of all, and we have one flag and one people.

In addition to the music, there were several speeches given by dignitaries, as well as opportunities for the veterans to share their stories. Songs were sung by the Maids of Honor of the William McKnight Camp, which was named for a local outstanding Confederate soldier. The Maids of Honor were dressed in beautiful white dresses and were met with great cheers and hand clapping. The southern belles from Winnsboro were Catherine Campbell, Craggy Morris, Cora Thompson, Nona Morris, and Willie Jones. When the group sang "Song of the South," it brought tears to many a dim eye.

On the last day of the reunion, a Thursday, there were about eight thousand in attendance as more soldiers of the gray joined their comrades. Six thousand pounds of beef had been barbecued for the occasion and dinner was ample. After meetings of the brigades, visitors were entertained with a delightful concert by the Andrews Band, and there was some fine old time dancing on the platform by many of the soldiers.

The presentation of the flag, a gift to the McKnight Camp, was made by Cora Thompson, sponsor of the camp. She was surrounded by her Maids of Honor, all dressed in snow white.

After the dinner and the concert and a few hours spent as veterans relived past experiences, "the long roll" was beat by A. D. Rape, a drummer boy during the Civil War. He never forgot how to beat a charge, and those who knew him in those days say he never learned how to beat a retreat. At the last roll of the drum, the crowd began to disperse, many never to meet again.

**The last Confederate Soldier**

This is the story of one of the last soldiers who wore the color of gray from 1861 to 1865. Most of those who pledged their allegiance to the Confederate states of America were farm boys from the old South. They did not know much about the Military Manual of Arms, but most could hit a tree knot up to one hundred yards away with their squirrel guns. One of these soldiers, Samuel M. Raney, was born on March 14, 1847, in Lincoln County, Tennessee. He received a limited education and worked on the family farm until the age of fifteen, when he entered the Confederate Army in June 1862. He served as a private in Company C 34th Regiment, Tennessee Infantry.

Private Raney was a fife player in the regimental band, but indicated his first responsibility was as a fighting soldier in the Confederate Army. Like many soldiers, he never got the bitterness of the bloody conflict out of his mind. Private Raney participated in several major battles; Bull Run, Cumberland Gap, Cannaway, and Murfreesboro.

After the battle of Bentonville, Gen. Joseph Johnson surrendered the regiments to Sherman at Durham, North Carolina on April 26, 1865. The Confederate soldiers marched to Chesapeake Bay, Maryland, and received little food or water. Private Raney was held in that prisoner of war camp until he and the other Confederate soldiers were paroled May 6, 1865.

The months following were a trying time for the Confederate soldiers. Many of them had not eaten in days and suffered from dysentery. They wore ragged clothes, had no money, and had only the long walk from Maryland back to their homes. Living like animals, remnants of the once proud Confederate Army made it home after weeks and months of starvation and tireless journey.

Raney returned to his home in Murfreesboro, not as the carefree young boy who had enlisted in 1862, but as a battle-scarred man would never be the same again. Jobs were scarce in Tennessee and across the south. Everything had been destroyed and the economy was in ruin. Many families had lost members in the war, homes and barns had been burned, and there was no money for planting crops or rebuilding.

After several weeks, Sam Raney found employment, working for a water canal project on the Tennessee River. Later, he moved to Alabama, but found economic conditions there similar to that of Tennessee. He started farming, and in 1870 married Mahala Gain Cagle in Lawrence, Alabama. After nine years living in Alabama, the couple migrated to Texas, settling at Palo Pinto in Stevens County. The land was rich and cheap, ideal for an Alabama farmer, but Sam had a yearning for a land of trees, hills, and streams of running water similar to Tennessee and Alabama.

In 1901, Sam and Mahala relocated to East Texas near Clarksville, later moving to the Majors Community east of Purley in Franklin County. There, he continued to farm as long as health permitted.

Whenever the boys in gray held a muster in neighboring cities, Raney would be there swapping stories with comrades in arms. At the muster, he always spoke fondly of his commander, Gen. Benjamin Cheatham.

Private Raney died March 15, 1950, at the age of 103, as the last surviving Confederate soldier in Texas. He is buried at the Providence Cemetery, north of Purley in Franklin County. A flat marble Confederate headstone marks the location where the old soldier rests beside his wife, Mahala.

As an interesting side note to the story of that Confederate soldier is one about my great-grandfather, J. D. Martin, who had been a Union POW. He had fought in the last encounter of the Civil War, known as the Wilderness Campaign, and then surrendered with the Army of Northern Virginia. I was told of how Martin spoke of the long walk home and the deplorable conditions he experienced along the road to Alabama.

He left Virginia wearing ragged clothes and shoes that he had covered with tattered pieces of discarded cloth. He had no food to eat or weapons for protection. Bands of armed Confederate soldiers, mostly deserters, roamed the countryside, taking anything of value from homes or travelers and stealing any available livestock. Martin spoke of seeing sick Confederate soldiers beside the road who were dying from exposure. They would be begging for food or a drink of water, and most needed medical assistance. There were some who were missing a leg, and they would make use of a tree limb that acted as a crutch, enabling them to hobble along for a mile or two each day. There was little that any of the men to help each other.

My great-grandfather would talk about how he would arrive maybe fifty yards from a farmhouse and holler out to occupants, requesting a drink of water and a morsel of food. Some of the people in the farmhouse, probably out of fear, ordered vagrant soldiers to leave, but other brave souls allowed Confederate soldiers to sleep in the barn and offered an ear of field corn. When the men received no help from the farmers, they slept in the open, or under a tree, and their only food was edible grass, leaves, or fruit that they might find on a nearby tree or bush.

After many weeks of hardship, the weak and battered body of J. D. Martin returned to his home in Limestone County, Alabama. Like other soldiers across the ages, he would never be the same again.

## City Hall

Prior to 1924, Winnsboro did not have an official City Hall. Space where local government could be conducted would be leased from a downtown property owner. The city had a water sewer system and an efficient volunteer fire department. Garbage disposal, street maintenance, and water sewer repairs were done by two or three city employees. The equipment they used consisted of shovels, picks, and a horse-drawn machine to grade city streets. The town's jail was said to be a room approximately 18' x 18', located at the intersection of Franklin and Elm Streets.

In 1924, the city acquired a parcel of land at the southwest corner of Main and Broadway. In 1879, it had been the site of M. D. Carlock Sr.'s grocery store, where he also held court as Justice of the Peace for Wood County Precinct Four.

When the new City Hall building was completed, the first floor housed a small apartment for the town's only paid fireman, who also served as night watchman. There was also a public restroom for women and children, a fire station, and a new jail at the west end of the building. The second floor had an office at the east entrance for the city secretary to conduct the city's business. Another office was shared jointly by the mayor and city marshal, and there was a large open area that could seat more than two hundred people. That area served as the City Council chamber, courtroom, election polling place, and a town hall meeting place.

Before the public restroom was built in the new City Hall, members of the Edelweiss Club had recognized the need for a public facility for women and children in about 1920. Through the efforts of the club members, a public restroom was opened in the Andrews Building in 1920. Mrs. Thomas became the first matron of the new public facility, then after serving two years, her daughter, Alfa Thomas, took her place.

When the city found itself short of funds to sponsor a public restroom after the new City Hall had been built, the mayor and council members approached the Edelweiss Club with an offer to lease them a large room on the first floor at the northeast corner of the city council building for one dollar a year. Club members voted to accept the offer, and in January 1925, moved the public restroom to the new quarters.

The room was furnished with attractive wicker furniture, rocking chairs, a baby bed, dressing table, magazine rack, lavatory, commodes, and other features to make patrons feel comfortable. Miss Alfa Thomas continued as service matron until 1947, when failing health forced her to retire. Birdie Robertson then succeeded her as matron. Each Saturday afternoon during those early years, there might be a line of women and children extending into the street, just patiently waiting for their turn.

As the city began to modernize and gas stations had their own restrooms, the ladies' restroom at City Hall had fewer and fewer patrons. Then on June 1,

1959, the doors of the facility closed for the last time, after 39 years of service to Winnsboro. When Birdie Robertson turned out the lights for the last time, we were saying goodbye, as I often say in my stories, "to a page of local history."

The Edelweiss Club was organized for study and civic involvement in 1911. Its members have studied everything from Shakespeare to Robert Browning; Texas writers, poets and artists, and government from the local level to the national scene. Guest speakers have included educators, doctors, lawyers, ministers, historians, musicians, world travelers, and others from varied walks of life.

Club membership has been comprised of housewives, teachers, business and professional women, young and retired ladies. But all have had a common purpose: a civic responsibility and a desire to develop a better understanding of Winnsboro's culture. The club's name, Edelweiss, was chosen to honor the Alpine flower found on the highest mountain top in the Swiss Alps, and there is a reason why that name was selected. The flower symbolizes struggle, endurance, and achievement. After a little over a century, the Edelweiss Club remains an active and vital organization within this community.

## The 1940s, '50s, and '60s

Movies of today hardly resemble the picture show of yesterday. For example, in 1950, after entering the local State Theater and passing an admission ticket to the ticket taker, the aroma of popcorn began to fill one's nostrils. That may be the same as it is today, but back then, Cokes, popcorn, and candy were only five or ten cents an item.

During the summer months, movie theaters had a cooling system that lowered the inside temperature by ten to twenty degrees. Most movies were still in black and white, although there was the occasional Technicolor film. A perfect day for a teenager was a ticket to the movie, money for a soft drink, popcorn, and candy bar, and sitting in a cool room watching their favorite movie stars.

On Saturdays, the main attraction in town was the movie theater. Doors opened at one in the afternoon and the first showing was a Western, then at 10:30 p.m., the midnight show began, always to a full house, and usually lasted until after midnight. Most stores downtown stayed open until the start of the late show and restaurants remained open until the midnight show crowd left their favorite eating establishments between one or two in the morning. Even the barbershops remained open until eleven o'clock in the evening.

By the 1960s, the cinema began to lose its appeal. Most everyone had a television and kids had cars. Merchants did everything possible to support the State Theater by providing free admission tickets and other promotions, but it became a losing proposition. Whereas in the 1940s all seats were filled up with about five hundred patrons, in the '60s only twenty to twenty-five tickets were sold for a movie. The last managers of the State Theater were Ronnie and Brenda Shirley. After the theater closed, they remained in Winnsboro to help shape the town's future. Ronnie became Postmaster, and

Brenda was a vice president of First National Bank for many years.

A famous Winnsboro landmark was Dad Brewer's Café, where hamburgers cost only five-cents until 1940, then the price increased to ten cents. The late Ed Brewer called the restaurant Dad Brewer's Hamburger Joint. Ed said that at the end of a movie, as four hundred or more moviegoers began to exit the theater, Dad would open the front door of his Café, place onions on the hot grill, and turn on a large fan in the rear of the building. The smell of food filtered into the street and soon hungry customers occupied all stools and others were waiting for the next available seat. In 1942, after twenty years of making hamburgers, Dad Brewer sold his business.

The young couple who purchased the café were Ruell and Catherine Cain. They renamed the business Cain Grill and began a remodeling program installing the latest available restaurant fixtures. The opening of the grill was delayed for three years, as Ruell was away serving as a sergeant in the U.S. Army in the European theater during World War II. He returned home to Winnsboro in 1946, and served the community in many ways. He was a member of the Winnsboro volunteer fire department, a Sunday school teacher at First Baptist Church, owner of a variety store, operator of the State Theater, restaurant owner, and a civic leader who had a passion for guiding young people in the right direction.

There was a romance about Dad Brewer's Hamburger Joint and the Cain Grill that has remained in the memory of its customers of that era. The place, which was on the northwest corner of Main at Elm, is remembered as a "poor man's corner", a place to sit and visit with friends while watching vehicles pass on the street outside. Facts became blurred with time, stories became folklore, and now they are history.

While the young men might be hanging out at one of the diners, the young women in Winnsboro might be taking piano lessons from Willa Wilfong, who also taught the girls how to be ladies in classes known as "expressions." Each spring, Willa would hold a recital at the Central Christian Church, and Mary White was one of Mrs. Wilfong's last students.

My most vivid memory of Ruell Cain was his involvement in a project that had to do with providing teenagers a safe and useful place to hang out on Friday and Saturday nights. The Junior Chamber of Commerce, made up mostly of World War II veterans, approached the city with a plan to convert the lower floor of the Carnegie library into a youth center known as Teen Town. Initially, city officials turned down the proposal because the activities included dancing. However, the city finally relented and approved the project after being convinced that Teen Town would be properly chaperoned. The beloved Miss Artie Vickers agreed to serve as what might be called house mother. Every kid in town loved and respected Miss Artie.

Teen Town provided a safe haven for Winnsboro youth for over fifteen years.

## The Korean War

On June 20, 1950, North Korea invaded South Korea, which was the start of the Korean Conflict, which the Truman administration called a police action. The local boys continued going to the State Theater, watching news reels of Korean soldiers and civilians dying each day on the streets and fields of South Korea. Some of the young men were eighteen, and had registered for selective service, while others were only sixteen or seventeen. Some of the guys said they were going to join the army, others would wait until they were drafted. A seventeen-year-old friend of mine persuaded his parents to sign a waiver enabling him to join the Navy.

The conflict lasted until July 27, 1953, when the Armistice was signed. Korea might be described as America's political war. The unrest in the Korean peninsula, being neither at peace nor war, remains today after sixty-one years. Korea, like other American wars, had been costly with the number lives sacrificed and the billions of dollars spent. The casualties of the Korean War were high—nearly five million people died, and more than half were civilians. The rate of casualties was higher than World War II and Vietnam. Almost forty thousand Americans died, and one hundred thousand were wounded. Nearly eight thousand soldiers were reported missing in action and 1,400 soldiers were captured. South Korea reported 373,599 civilian and 137,899 military deaths. North Korea and China suffered staggering losses.

**Reflections of Winnsboro**

## Winnsboro's Civilian Conservation Corps

To provide jobs during the Great Depression, President Franklin D. Roosevelt created the Civilian Conservation Corps (CCC). He signed the CCC bill into law on March 31, 1933, soon after he was elected president. Initially, men between the ages of eighteen to twenty-five were employed in the program, that later the age was changed to include seventeen-year-olds. Regular and reserve officers from all branches of the service commanded the camps and the companies. By July of that year, thousands of Texas men were outfitted with World War I surplus uniforms and tents. CCC men cut mountain roads, dug earthen dams, made furniture, log cabins, and reclaimed unusable land.

Today, Texas still has thirty-one state parks that were constructed by the CCC.

Through the efforts of Judge Will Suiter, Winnsboro was selected as the site for a Black CCC camp. J. J. Carroll, owner of thirty-two acres of land east of present-day Gilbreath Memorial Library, leased ten acres to the U.S. government, and Camp SCS-22-T, Co. 2884 {c} was established on August 20, 1935.

Immediately, six barracks, a mess hall, bathhouse, recreation hall, headquarters, latrines, and water lines were constructed. The installation housed two hundred fifty enlisted men, two army officers, a doctor, eight teachers, and the six operation foremen. Captain Homer Fry was the first commanding officer, followed by Lieutenant John Sandford. Second Lieutenant N. J. McKendry served as second in command. Enrollees were physically fit and came from families that were on government relief. Each man earned thirty dollars a month, of which twenty-five dollars went directly to his family. The impact of monthly allotment checks to families was felt in the local economy throughout East Texas.

Life in the military-style camp settled into a regular routine, with men working in army fatigues every day except Sunday. On Sundays, they were given passes to town and had to pass inspection as they were required to wear dress uniforms and be spit-and-polished like the regular Army.

The men from the Winnsboro CCC accomplished a lot in the years they worked in an area of about a twenty-mile radius. They built fire lanes, participated in volunteer firefighting, planted trees, built fences, terraced land, built dams, and dealt with water conservation. Most men served the program for a two-year period, while others chose to extend their enrollment. Many young men had never left home before, and when terms were up, some chose to remain in the Winnsboro area and put down roots as successful citizens.

At this time, many men in the program were functionally illiterate. The CCC provided classes in English, spelling, arithmetic, writing, and vocational courses. Some enrollees received the equivalent of a high school education while in the program, and a few received college degrees. Many men took advantage of the opportunity to be in the CCC and have the chance to excel. The Winnsboro CCC camp continued operation until 1942, when manpower demands of World War II brought it to an end.

## Soda pop and bottling plants

Soda pop has satisfied thirst of Winnsboro folks since Ruben Campbell constructed the first ice plant at Freeze Springs in 1901. Later, in about 1914, Nathe Spearman operated the Winnsboro Bottling Company. The late Fern Gilbreath once visited with me about the summer that he worked as a bottle washer at the Winnsboro Bottling Company. Fern was paid ten cents an hour to wash the bottles that had been returned for a deposit. Each bottle was washed by hand with soap and water, placed on a tray to dry, then re-filled with a favorite beverage and sold.

The Bottling Works was located in the rear of what is now the Cowboy Way Bible Class building on 110 West Elm Street. Mr. Spearman had a café in the front part of the building, where he served a variety of different soda-water drinks to patrons. According to those who were there at the time, the café always had a full house of people eager to sample the different beverages. It seems that people could not get enough of the tasty drinks.

One summer, Mr. Spearman purchased a spring-stopper machine. It was thought to be a Hutchinson spring-stopper. The stopper bottle was opened by pushing down on a wire loop. When the gasket pushed down through a pressure release, it created a loud popping sound, and that is how soda pop received its name. At least, this is in an accepted version among some people. Other names of the beverage included mineral waters, soda water, and just plain pop.

The manufacture of soda water started about 1835, and was mostly produced by the fountain-type equipment; bottling plants were few in numbers. By 1895, more plants were built, primarily in the Northeast. Hand-blown glass bottles were used, and finding methods to seal the bottles was an early challenge. Companies that manufactured bottled soda water were at first only in the metropolitan areas of the East and Midwest. Several years passed before the South would attain a position of prominence in the bottling industry.

In the early twentieth century, few bottlers had the knowledge to properly preserve the liquid in a bottle. When bottling companies acquired a machine that would seal bottles by pressure and a release mechanism, business began to boom. The five-cent drink was refreshing, especially after the introduction of ice to cool the liquid in the summer. Another bottling plant was located at 312 North Main, in the rear of the building where Network Technologies is located today. It is thought to have operated here for two or three years before moving on. Then the building housed the Shelton Bank, the Cain Bank, and later became the Post Office.

Spearman sold his bottling business to Mr. Craddock, and the business moved to the rear of a building at 200 Market Street, where the Lone Star Steakhouse is today. The Craddock Bottling Company faced Franklin Street, and it is thought that it operated from World War I until 1921. The late Carl Gilbreath, younger brother of Fern Gilbreath and a longtime

## Reflections of Winnsboro

Winnsboro barber, worked for Mr. Craddock as a bottle washer in 1917 and 1918. The Craddock Bottling Company was a franchise business that bottled Coca-Cola drinks, as well as a variety of other soda refreshments.

Carl described the plant as having large barrels of different kinds of flavored syrup suspended overhead on a screen plank, with a hose leading from each barrel containing the ingredients for the drinks. Below the platform was a conveyor belt where the bottles were placed. The mixing process involved placing the exact amount of syrup mixture into each bottle, followed by carbonated water, then the bottler placed a cap on the bottle. The employees had to be careful to get the mixture just right, and if they didn't, Mr. Craddock would let them know of his displeasure.

Craddock sold his Coca-Cola bottling plant to a group of businessmen from Pittsburg, Texas in early 1920s, where it continued for the next forty years.

The last soft drink bottling business in Winnsboro was located on West Broadway, where the First Baptist Church parking lot is today. After World War II, Babe Bryce and David Steed operated a bottling plant there. Babe and David sold a variety of bottled drinks, including one they called Squirt. The business did not last long, however the drink Squirt survived and has received wide distribution over the years by another bottler. Once they told me, "you can lose your shirt fast in the cold drink business."

## Chapter Sixteen – Famous People From Winnsboro

Remembering someone from your youth that you joked with, sat beside in Tubby Smith's American History class, played ping-pong with at Teen Town, and now, after many years attempting to honor her in written words, is a bittersweet memory.

This is a story about Jonan Brown Williams, remembered as a dear friend from the past, who contracted the most dreaded disease of the 1950s—polio. After experiencing a serious setback like that, most people would have given up; however, Jonan was an inspiration, as she had things to do over the next thirty years. This story is not about the hardships she faced, but what she would want to be remembered for, her family and her accomplishments.

Jonan was born January 25, 1931, in Oil City, Louisiana and spent her early years at Vivian, Louisiana. Her parents, John and Bee Brown, moved to Winnsboro in 1945, accompanied by their daughter. This was the height of the oil boom, so living accommodations were scarce, but the family finally located an apartment. Later, a house at 206 South Mill Street became available for rent. John, an employee of Magnolia oil company, bought the house, and members of the Brown family would remain at that address for the next half-century.

Bee was a sweet and caring mother who remained her daughter's best friend throughout their lives. Bee was a wonderful seamstress who kept her daughter dressed in the latest fashions. John, Bee, and Jonan were devout Methodists, and, when the church doors opened, they were always there. After John retired from the oil company, he was a volunteer custodian at his church the First United Methodist Church of Winnsboro.

Jonan attended Winnsboro High School, and she had a certain humorous wit about her that other students seemed to appreciate. She was active in extracurricular activities, serving on the *Raider* and *Tomahawk* staff, as a member of the Spanish Club, Choral Club, Pep Squad, and as a class officer. Teachers were fond of this outgoing young lady, and everyone liked the girl with the big smile. Thinking back, I guess journalism and theater were her major loves in high school.

After graduating high school in 1949, Jonan attended Texas State College for Women, which is now TWU in Denton. After graduating there in 1952, she completed graduate work in journalism at SMU and at the University of Oklahoma. She was a speech and theater teacher for two years in the Dallas Independent school District. During this time, Jonan married and had a daughter, Lynan.

In 1957, after contracting polio, Jonan returned to Winnsboro with her eighteen- month-old daughter. At that time, Jonan was in an iron lung machine and endured months of physical hardship and physical therapy. She also endured a divorce.

Jonan did not let her physical limitations hold her back. Despite the fact that she was confined to a wheelchair and had only the use of two fingers with which to write or paint, as soon as she was able, she got very involved in community organizations. She was a member of the Winnsboro League of Arts from the beginning and took every art class that was offered. She won numerous community service awards and honors: Rotary Citizenship Award in 1964; Chamber of Commerce R. H. McCrary Award, which was the Winnsboro's Woman of the Year in 1973; Winnsboro League of Arts Award in 1977. In 1980, and 1987, she was recognized by the Autumn Trails Association for her twenty-one years of service as editor and writer of the Autumn Trails brochure.

It was Jonan's tradition to write a descriptive essay about autumn in each annual edition of the brochure, and she always took pride in conducting a beautiful, professionally-judged Autumn Trails Queens pageant. She was director of the pageant for seventeen years. Jonan once told her daughter Lynan, "It does not matter what you do for others just as long as you do something. And that you contribute as you are able."

In speaking of her mother Lynan said, "I never thought of mother as disabled, only inconvenienced."

In 1962, at the fourth Autumn Trails Festival, Jonan presented her play "The Cabin," a story that touched on the history of East Texas from 1850 to the '60s. Drama critics from The Dallas Morning News hailed her play as exceptionally good, and after the Winnsboro production the play was performed at Texas Woman's University in Denton and received good reviews. In October, 2011, The Winnsboro Center for the Arts had an exhibit of Jonan's paintings and mounted her play "The Cabin" as a special tribute during that year's Autumn Trails events. On Saturday,

**Reflections of Winnsboro**

Oct 22, 2011 members of the Winnsboro High School class of 1949 were invited to a reception at the art center to honor the memory of Jonan Brown Williams as part of the annual class reunion.

My last visit with Bee Brown, just before she sold her home, was a mixture of sadness and happiness. As we talked, we both laughed about happy events, high school friends, parties, and the time I stepped on Jonan's foot while dancing. My eyes were a bit teary as we talked about it all, as well as the memories in that historic home that they lived in. That visit with Bee is a cherished memory; she was a classy lady.

## Claudia Cranston

The name Claudia Cranston does not ring a bell with most Winnsboro area citizens, but in the 1920s and 1930s, the name was familiar to Americans, especially in New York City where she was a magazine writer and author.

Claudia was a descendent of George and Lucinda Cranston, who established Cranston Pottery on East Pine Street and had a son, Christopher Columbus Cranston, who was born in 1862. He was remembered as a potter, hunter, and dog trainer, and he enjoyed living in the great outdoors. Christopher and his wife, Esther, had four children: Olive, Claudia, John, and Loma.

Claudia was born in 1887 in Denton, Texas, and came to Winnsboro as a young child. Claudia attended school at Winnsboro's Texas Collegiate Institute, the school that was built in 1888 west of

Walker Park. Since Winnsboro did not have a high school at that time, she returned to Denton for advanced studies. After completion of some college work, this aspiring young lady headed east to Washington D.C., first obtaining government employment. This talented girl from Winnsboro might be described as someone seeking to see the world, meet exciting people, and record their images.

After a successful time in Washington, Claudia moved to the Big Apple—New York City—and became a fashion copywriter for Vogue Magazine. Dobbs Ferry Road on the Hudson River became her home. Her inspiration and motivation to write novels came while viewing ships traveling the mighty Hudson, and the beautiful countryside propelled a desire to share her thoughts. By 1922, her works were featured in several magazines. She accepted a commission to tour Europe and write about its people, their problems, and share their customs. After returning to New York City, Claudia joined Atlantic Monthly as a feature writer. By this time, fame and fortune had reached the girl from Winnsboro.

In 1934, Claudia again said goodbye to New York City. She accepted a commission from Good Housekeeping Magazine to tour the South Pacific. Her assignment was to write stories about the past and all the exotic places, which she did in serial form. Her descriptions of the lands and islands, the people and their habitat, became the image of this faraway part of the world for many Americans. Her stories of travel and adventure excited the American public. She returned to New York from the South Pacific in 1935, and completed her most famous story, *Sky Gypsy*. It told of her five-thousand-mile trip by plane to places in Mexico, South America, and the Caribbean.

Then, once again, Cranston returned to Europe in 1936, visiting all countries except the Soviet Union. Her travel book *I've Been Around* was born at this time and published in 1938. This was the seventh book that she had written. Besides the travel tales, she wrote two mystery novels, *Maritime Murder* and *Murder on Fifth Avenue*. She also wrote two other novels, *Ready to Wear* and *Part Time Girl*, as well as a book on parties entitled *How to Entertain*.

Good Housekeeping Magazine persuaded the famous writer to accept another assignment to Europe to view the continent's worrisome problems as clouds of war gathered. She found most of the people she met were living a carefree life and not concerned about the war, but she did consider Hitler a tyrant. Claudia completed her assignment and returned to the United States before war began in 1939.

Claudia's work that I remember most is *Rosiki The Rose*. In 1949, MGM acquired the film rights and produced a successful movie titled, "It's a Big Country." The movie was shown here in Winnsboro at the State Theatre, and most of the townspeople stood in line for a seat to view the film based on a book written by a hometown girl.

By then Claudia was an associate editor at Good Housekeeping and had contributed articles, short stories, and poetry to many other national magazines, including Ladies' Home Journal and Atlantic Monthly.

In about 1940, Claudia Cranston returned to the Orient. She said, "We have buried our heads like an ostrich and assumed the East does not exist. We have yet to learn that we cannot ignore the problems of the Orient, the situation must be faced and the sooner we face it the better."

Well, like the ostrich we did keep our heads buried in the sand until December 7, 1941.

Claudia returned to her Winnsboro home in 1946, a tired and sick adventurer who had traveled the world for forty years.

After experiencing a rich life filled with the excitement and fame, this world-famous writer, who understood the meaning of words, died on June 27, 1970. Her funeral was conducted at her childhood church, Central Christian Church, and she is buried in City Cemetery in Winnsboro.

## Bama Pies

Many people don't know it, but the founders of the successful Bama Pie Company came from Winnsboro. In the early 1900s, Henry Marshall was an unsuccessful farmer in the area, and he finally gave up farming and made plans to go to Dallas. Henry sent his wife, Bama, and seven children to Dallas in an iron-rimmed wagon while he stayed behind to sell his stock, tools, and anything else he had to pay his debts. Then he, too, headed for Dallas, walking and picking cotton and hitching rides.

Meanwhile, Bama got a job in Dallas, cooking at a Woolworth diner, and one of her specialties was a little pie that customers loved. In about 1930, Henry urged her to make the pies at home so he could sell them door to door, which he did to great success. As the business grew, Henry bought an old Ford car that became the Bama Pie Company's first delivery car. After a time, Bama quit her job at Woolworth's, and, with the help of the children, started producing hundreds of the little pies a day. An agreement with McDonald's to supply pies to the various franchises across the country launched the Bama Pie Company into prominence.

## Chapter Seventeen - The Building of the Arts District

**It started with an old city tradition**

When I was boy of ten or twelve years of age, the big event for most of the locals was the Fourth of July Fiddling Contest at City Park. It was held at the Pavilion, a large wooden structure located south of the present City Auditorium. The building had large shutters over open windows that could be raised to permit light and fresh air to filter inside. Wooden benches were placed across the room facing a stage.

During the contest, all benches were filled by spectators, and several hundred others would be standing inside and outside the building as the bands performed. Among those that were watching, you might have seen one man dressed in a suit and tie while another would be wearing a blue work shirt, overalls, and brogan shoes. Filled with hundreds of perspiring man women and children, the Pavilion always seemed to be warm during the Fourth of July festivities. The building didn't have air conditioning or electric fans, but I guess you never missed what you never had in the first place.

When politicians and entertainers came to town, the public building served as a civic center. It also once served as the high school gym for basketball and as the National Guard Armory. From 1926 to 1950, many local and state political figures addressed enthusiastic audiences from the speaker's podium at the Pavilion.

### Reflections of Winnsboro

With heavy traffic, sand as fine as powder would filter through the air at City Park. Members of Company K of the National Guard handled traffic control and parking for the crowd that sometimes swelled to five or six thousand people. This swimming pool, commonly called the "Nat," would be overflowing with swimmers. Visitors would bring their own food for the day, but they could also enjoy watermelon, popcorn, soda pop, and snow cones that were available for five cents each. Usually, a fireworks display would be held the night before the Fourth of July event, compliments of local merchants.

The fiddlers first started gathering at the Pavilion in 1926, and then in 1927, they officially organized and named the event the Fourth of July Fiddlers Convention. The first celebration drew a crowd of four thousand people, and the bands that performed were from Winnsboro, Oak Grove, Yantis, Coke, and Cumby, including the Attaway Band.

L. M. Gilbreath served as the organization's first president and extended an invitation to Tri-County residents to come for an enjoyable time, where they could listen to good music and share plenty of cool water, swim in a fine natatorium, or lounge under shade trees.

By the second event, Winnsboro had its own band under the direction of C. A. Hewitt, the local high school's first band director.

In 1932, five thousand people were on hand to greet the fiddlers and listen to a speech by Mayor C. M. Cain. Then in 1933, the number of bands was limited to fifteen, and seven prizes were given in cash and merchandise to the contestants. A huge crowd of six thousand was on hand, which was the largest crowd to attend any event at City Park.

The 1930s were exciting years for the fiddlers. Times were tough and money was tight, but this leisure time represented an outlet for folks who were struggling to survive during the Great Depression years.

In 1940, the organizing committee of the Fiddler Convention decided not to give prizes to contestants. This was a mistake, because fewer bands and smaller crowds started showing up for the annual Fourth of July celebration. The following year, a committee of local businessmen—Tobe Wright, Leroy Hawkins, and Barney Dodgen—raised a considerable amount of money for the thirteen participating bands. Under the leadership of these men, the event experienced great success as thousands once again gathered for the Fourth of July celebration.

During World War II, the association decided to cancel the event for the duration of the war. Uncle Sam had decreed that wartime work must not be interrupted.

The two years following the end of the war were not good years for the fiddlers, but that soon changed. Fiddlers once again came back to the park, and by 1949, the Fourth of July Fiddlers Convention was again a front-page story with a new breed of fiddlers. That year, the audience exceeded three thousand. A. H. Attaway took the first-place prize and J. T. Hayes came in second.

In 1950, Thurman Polk became president of the organization, with Buddy Faulk as a sponsor. Area merchants offered generous support of the fiddlers and the event, and it continued for a number of years.

Sadly, in 1986, the Old Fiddler's Association ceased to function after being a successful part of Winnsboro's social history for nearly sixty years through donations from generous folks living in the Winnsboro area. What killed this long-running production? Seems that someone came up with the bright idea to charge people five dollars to enter City Park for the event.

When the Old Fiddlers played their last tune, and turned off the lights, a way of life disappeared in Winnsboro.

## Winnsboro Renaissance

Changes came to downtown Winnsboro in April of 1995, when Barbara Hums and Barb Richert opened The Winnsboro Bakery, after completely renovating the old Cain Bank on North Main Street. Energetic entrepreneurs with a great interest in art, they not only changed the image of a small-town diner into an upscale eating establishment, they adorned the walls with fine art, offered pieces for sale, and occasionally sponsored live music. Not only were they committed to making a success of their business, they were dedicated to their new home and worked tirelessly to promote The Winnsboro Bakery and the town of Winnsboro.

"The Barbaras" as they were to be affectionately called, operated the bakery until August of 2004, when they sold it to Jeff Heath, who eventually added a saloon and an outdoor patio, where he hosted live music. Both women stayed in Winnsboro for a number of years and were supporters of the Winnsboro Center For the Arts, serving on the board of directors at different times. Barbara Richert has become a pastel artist of considerable renown, and she moved to Lufkin some years ago. However, she continues to support the Winnsboro Center For the Arts and often comes back to visit.

Jeff Heath likewise was a supporter of the art center, where he served on the board of directors and volunteered in a number of capacities. Like so many of the people who have come to Winnsboro after retiring from corporate positions elsewhere, Jeff has an interest in art and let that interest blossom through photography, graphic art, and music.

Other people who influenced the early years of the Winnsboro Renaissance were Dub and Lori Forsyth, who opened Main Street Gallery in the late '90s. The store had fine art for sale, as well as specialty craft items, and the couple often joined me on the historical walking tours that the Preservation League sponsored.

The Winnsboro Gallery, owned by Mary and Jim Smith, opened on Main Street in September 2007, and offered fine art for sale, as well as framing services. It was in business until March 2010. The back part of the building was renovated and turned into an upscale coffee shop, Art & Espresso, that Marilyn Arnaud and her husband, Jim Hollowell, purchased on April 1, 2009. Local artists could have pieces on the wall for sale, and a number of those fine art paintings were sold. Marilyn operated the coffee shop at that first site on Market Street until July 2013, when the shop moved to the corner of Market and Broadway, at the former Lou Viney location. The coffee shop stayed open there until March 31, 2016.

Much like its predecessor, Lou Viney, Art & Espresso was a gathering place for people, not unlike the diners of the '30s and '40s. People would come to eat or get a cup of coffee, and stay for a while to visit. According to Marilyn it was "a place where strangers came in and went out with new friends. It was even romantic. So many people had first dates there. Met their future spouses and then a couple of years later brought in their newborns."

## The Music Festival

During this time of cultural renewal in Winnsboro, another music tradition was born. In the year 2000, a group of interested music lovers gathered at the Oakley mansion with the idea of planning how to share the gift of music with the community. This group founded a nonprofit organization called the Northeast Texas Music Festival, and its lofty goal was to make Winnsboro the music capital of East Texas. Officers of this organization were Norma Wilkinson, Duane Redding, and Henry Spiva. Art Greenhaw, Grammy Award winner and member of the Light Crust Doughboys, donated his time and expertise to the organization. Rev. Henry Suche, Dan Noteware, Mike Crouch, and the late Barney Anderson served as outstanding directors over the years.

The first year of the Music Fest was 2001, and it was held at City Park. The late Richard Foster, owner of the local radio station KWNS-FM, did a masterful job producing the three-day event. He was assisted by Randy Lindsey and Norma Wilkinson. Another creative member of the production team was author Helen Myers, who served as communications director.

That was an exciting beginning for the festival. The three-day event featured Janie Fricke, Gene Watson, and country-western favorite Dan Seals. Others who offered flavor to the festival were Karen Taylor-Good, Terri Hendrix, Darrell Luster, Lloyd Maines, and many other music greats.

Producer Sonny Foster took over the reins from his father Richard Foster, and donated his time and talent to produce some of the best shows in East Texas for the next seven years. Those people who formed the organization and donated so much of their time, talent, and treasure are owed a debt of gratitude for what they did to make this event successful.

## The Winnsboro Center For the Arts

**This section, and The Bowery Stage section, was written by Maryann Miller, based on facts related by Bill Jones, Lynn Adler, Lindy Hearne, and Jim Willis; and taken from the WCA History documents.**

To ascertain the current and future needs of the people in the community, the City of Winnsboro conducted a series of town hall meetings in 2000, with the assistance of the Texas Rural Commission. In the spring of 2001, the Commission provided a comprehensive report that identified two underserved groups in this region—senior/retired citizens and school-age children. The report also showed a lack of cultural arts and community programming for both groups.

A group of citizens who had attended one or more of the town hall meetings continued to get together over a period of several months to develop the concept of an all-inclusive art center to meet those identified needs. The Trails Country Center for the Arts (TCCA) was formed, with a board of directors comprised of artists, writers, educators, business executives, and community leaders. Al and Myrna Stillman, Al and Ila Moore, Rod and Georgia Lange, Carolyn Jones, Dick and Betty Groper, and Tracy Hopkins were part of the original group to do strategic planning. Dick Groper wrote the original bylaws, and Ila Moore completed the paperwork to apply for the Federal and State tax-exempt status.

The Stillmans bought the building at 200 Market Street, and made it available to the newly-organized art center to rent, eventually arranging for the organization to purchase the building.

"Al Stillman had the fire for rejuvenating the downtown area," Lynn Adler said in an interview. "I called him 'The Baron of the Bowery' because he did so much to bring new businesses and art to the community."

In the early years of making the building usable as an art center, many people contributed time and money and expertise. Just a few of those were Al Moore, Al Stillman, John and Patty Burke, and Bill Jones. The roof needed to be fixed, new wiring had to be put in, and bathrooms installed. That first renovation was done with limited funds, but soon the space was ready for some classes and concerts.

The Trails Country Playhouse made a contribution of $800 to the original funding of TCCA. That was a troupe of players in Winnsboro that had in its membership Brandon Franks, Mike and Shannon Monk, Rod and Georgia Lange, Helen Burlingham, Jennifer Blair, Austin Johnson, Judy Valentine, John Gore, Tina Hammer, Anne Reeves, and many more.

Singer/songwriters Lindy Hearne and Lynn Adler were also an important part of the first years of TCCA, and continue as supporters. Lindy started coming to Winnsboro from Fort Worth in 2000, and singer/songwriter Starr Perry introduced him to Norma Wilkerson, who asked him to be an advisor for the Music Festival. Norma hosted several concerts at her B&B, the Oaklea Mansion, and Lindy assisted in getting talent such as Ruthie Foster and Steve Young to perform.

Soon, Lynn Adler joined Lindy in Winnsboro, and the couple bought property that had been owned by Joseph and Mary Germann. They call their place in the country the Spring Hollow Organic Song Farm, and have written a number of songs celebrating Winnsboro and East Texas. To help the art center get established, the duo generously donated their talent for concerts and coordinated a songwriters' workshop. They arranged for Miranda Lambert to do a benefit concert, and then had her come to do another concert the following year. She was only 17sseventeen years old at the time, and she invited another East Texas singer, Kacey Musgraves, to open for her.

According to Lindy, things really got rolling after that. The next major talent to appear at TCCA was Ray Wylie Hubbard. That concert was co-sponsored with Jeff Heath, who had dinner at The Winnsboro Bakery and people came across the street for the show.

In 2008 and 2009, representatives from TCCA took responsibility for the Cultural Enrichment segment of the 21st Century After-School Program at Memorial Middle School, which was serving seventy at-risk students. Classes in writing, art, drama, photography, dance, and music were conducted starting in November, and ran through the end of the school year. Art classes were conducted by Graham Hopkins and Georgia Moore. Maryann Miller led the drama and writing classes with Georgia Moore, and dance classes were led by Laurel Cox. Other classes were led by Cindy Fischer. Dance, art, and drama classes for children and adults were also held at the art center, with tap-dancing lessons taught by June Hamilton.

In 2008, TCCA was renamed the Winnsboro Center for the Arts (WCA), and the organization has grown from its humble beginning in 2001 to a vibrant cultural center that continues to attract new volunteers and has developed an aggressive schedule of events in all mediums of artistic endeavor. It is the cornerstone of the Cultural Arts District, a designation given to the city in 2009, and when Anita Perry spoke at the Depot in March of 2003 to honor the city's being named a Main Street City, she cited the art center as one of the three most valuable resources in Winnsboro, the other two being Lou Viney and The Winnsboro Bakery.

The WCA is supported 100 percent through volunteer efforts and offers a wide range of programming in all area of creative interest from fine art to folk art, music, drama, literary events, and classes and workshops. It has also fostered original theatre productions such as "There is A Time," written by Maryann Miller; "King Kong, The Musical," written by Bob Hibbard; "Bonnie & Clyde in Winnsboro," written by Randy Lindsey, and the KidZZ on Stage Summer Drama Camp musical productions. The musical shows for drama camp have been led by Dallas-based singer/songwriter George Gagliardi, vocalist Shannon Monk, music teacher Jennifer Zimmerman, Hayley Morris, Cassia Rose, and Vivien Tagg.

There is not another art center in the surrounding five-county area that is that inclusive of all forms of artistic expression and offers both classes and opportunities to perform or take part in an exhibition in the gallery. Exhibits such as Women in the Arts and Men in the Arts, mounted by Brenda Roberts, celebrate the artistic achievements of men and women in the Winnsboro area and beyond.

WCA sponsors the Annual Trails Country Treasure Award, and in 2007, Bill Jones was honored for his many contributions to the center as a valued advisor and volunteer, as well as for his dedication to preserving the history of Winnsboro and Wood County. He jokes that he was the maintenance man for the art center for many years, fixing things, as well as assisting in the first restoration of the historic building, offering his expertise and contacts for roof repair and other construction needs. He was also an advisor on the plans for selling the 204 building, and was instrumental in managing the eventual sale.

Trails Country Treasure Award winners in order: Odenna Brannan, 2006; Bill Jones, 2007; George and LaVonna Hitz, 2008; Helen Burlingham, 2009; Graham Hopkins, 2010; Maryann Miller, 2011; Lynn Adler and Lindy Hearne, 2012; J. T. Mullinax, 2013; Al and Georgia Moore, 2014; Becky Pickett, 2015; Joe Dan Boyd, 2016.

## Crossroads Music Company & Listening Room

In November, 2005, Lindy Hearne and Lynn Adler, the singing duo Adler & Hearne, established the live music venue Crossroads Music Company & Listening Room at the site of the former McCrary's Hardware Store and Soda Shop. They hosted national touring artists on a weekly basis—artists that you could see in Dallas or Houston or other big cities could now be seen in Winnsboro.

Entertainers performed on the Front Porch Stage, which Lindy built with old wood and siding from a garage in Corsicana. The stage, which was built to look like an actual front porch on a country home, was a hit with audience members, as well as the musicians who came to play on a Friday or Saturday night. Friday nights were often open mic nights, where local talent was encouraged to come and gain some experience playing in front of a live audience. On some Sunday afternoons, local pastors would bring their youth groups to play on the front porch stage.

Just a few of the many performers who graced the stage during the three years Crossroads was led by Adler & Hearne were Billy Joe Shaver, Ralph Stanley and The Clinch Mountain Boys, Ruthie Foster, Kinky Friedman, Ray Wylie Hubbard, Terri Hendrix and Lloyd Maines, and Kacey Musgraves. Kate Hearne, Lindy's daughter who is now establishing her own music career, was starting to play guitar and sing during that time, and she would often get tips from the musicians on chord changes and guitar riffs. Kate was thrilled when Kacey Musgraves asked her to open for her.

Crossroads Music Company & Listening Room was always popular with people who have weekend homes near one of the area lakes, and it received a big boost when Michael Grandberry from the Dallas Morning News started giving the venue coverage. He was a fan of Jimmy LaFave, and when Michael got word that Jimmy was going to perform live in Winnsboro, he came to see him. Michael was so impressed with Crossroads, and the Front Porch Stage, he continued to give mention of upcoming events in the music section of The Dallas Morning News.

Other support also came from The County Line Magazine, and publisher P. A. Geddie and her brother, Tom Geddie, were often seen in the audience.

In May of 2009, Lynn and Lindy turned leadership of Crossroads over to Stephen Marshall, who moved the venue across Market Street to the Winnsboro Center for the Arts. Stephen had hopes of raising money to renovate the 204 Market Street building that WCA owned as a performance space. When funding for that project did not come through, Stephen passed

**Reflections of Winnsboro**

the reins to Gus Gustafson in 2010, who produced a number of concerts at WCA before taking Crossroads to Sulphur Springs.

## The Bowery Stage

For the years it operated, Crossroads Music Company & Listening Room made the city a destination for live music. It was unique because it was a true listening room—not a venue where you listened to music while you ate or drank, but one where the music itself was the reason for being there. In 2013, Gus Gustafson and Crossroads was being courted by the city of Sulphur Springs, and after a banner year in Winnsboro, Gus made the decision to move. This left Winnsboro without a comparable listening-room venue.

At the same time, the WCA was in the middle of remodeling and restoring their building, and as part of that project, the stage was redesigned and rebuilt. A Blue Lite lighting system was installed, and the sound system was upgraded with a new mixer. The WCA Board of Directors decided that it should take action to fill the void left by Crossroads, and The Bowery Stage was born, with Jim Willis being named to manage it.

The first concert was held April 27, 2014, shortly after the remodeled WCA reopened, and the artists were Winnsboro's own Adler & Hearne. There were ten more concerts that year, with most of the earlier ones being performers that had played Crossroads previously, such as Ray Wylie Hubbard. As Jim Willis and the board learned more about the business, they began moving in a slightly different direction with music; more toward the folk genre and less toward blues, though still keeping a strong presence of traditional singer/songwriters. Michael Jonathon (PBS Woodsongs radio host), Michael (Bluer than Blue) Johnson, and Joe Crookston were the first performers that were more in the folk genre.

The booking of Michael Johnson was the event that turned efforts toward performers of the '60's and '70's. Jim Willis began establishing a relationship with Tamulevich Artist Management, and it was through them that Peter Yarrow was booked for two sold-out nights in May 2015. The Bowery Stage at the Winnsboro Center for the Arts was already riding the high reputation set by Crossroads, and had the added benefit of being a 501(c)(3). Booking Yarrow raised the venue to another level. Shortly afterwards, when Uncle Calvin's Coffeehouse, one of the highest profile folk music venues in Dallas, was trying to bring Melanie to their stage, they called on WCA to partner with them and the tour was arranged. Following those successful concerts, The Bowery Stage was able to arrange, in short order, concerts by Michael Martin Murphey, Tom Paxton, and Judy Collins.

In 2014 and 2015, there were two concerts featuring classical guitar, and in 2016, that interest in classical music led to a four-concert subscription series called the Sunday Classical Series. Artists were opera and symphony members; soloists, principals, and concertmaster. The quality of music was high, attendance was high, and the series was very successful. Performance schedules for concerts in 2017, and beyond, will include some classical musicians.

# Reflections of Winnsboro

The Bowery Stage venue is noted for its excellent sound and appreciative and knowledgeable audiences. Coupled with the welcoming town of Winnsboro, it is becoming a very desired tour-stop for performers. The Bowery Stage is upgrading the sound system with new powered monitors, new powered, flying FOS speakers, and one of the finest digital sound boards available. Artists smile when they hear that, and, as the reputation of the Bowery Stage continues to grow, more and more great artists will come to Winnsboro.

The cost of the concerts is partially covered by sponsors, local businesses and individuals, and Jim Willis, along with the Board of Directors at the Winnsboro Center for the Arts, is very grateful for the support of the many friends, sponsors, and members, who continue to help keep the arts alive in East Texas.

## ABOUT THE AUTHOR

Throughout his whole life, Bill Jones has always been interested in history. He jokes that his love of history started in high school because it was so easy to get an "A" in the class. He went on to study history and government at East Texas Commerce, and eventually taught school in Longview and El Paso.

Bill came back to his hometown of Winnsboro in 1981, wanting to get back to his roots, and he formed the Preservation League in 1983. The first historical marker was placed at the intersection of Main and Pine Streets, where the town of Crossroads, later to become Winnsboro, was established.

Since then, Bill has placed over 35 historical markers around the East Texas area to inform visitors of important historic events such as the many visits by Bonnie and Clyde, the shoot-out on Market Street—when it was the Bowery—and the dedication of the Railroad Depot. Those markers have included Texas Historical Markers, Wood County Historical Markers, and City of Winnsboro Historical Markers.

Bill was one of the founders of the Rock Gym Preservation Committee and was instrumental in saving that beautiful old building.

In 1983, Bill was the chairman of the Winnsboro Historical Society, and in 1990 he became President of the Wood County Historical Society, a position he held for ten years. Through all of those associations, Bill gathered stories about the people and places and events that are significant to Winnsboro through interviews with descendants of early settlers, as well as detailed research. He put those stories in columns that he wrote for *The Wood County Democrat, The Winnsboro News, The Center Fold*, a newspaper for the Winnsboro Senior Citizens' Center; and a newsletter for the Winnsboro Area Chamber of Commerce. He also had a monthly radio show, "Look Back in History," on KWNS 104.7FM, a Winnsboro radio station, and contributed articles to *Texas Highways Magazine* and *Big "D" Magazine*.

Bill continues to be active in community events, especially those dealing with history.

~ ~ ~ ~ ~ ~ ~ ~

Maryann Miller is a freelance writer and editor, as well as the author of numerous books. She has written for, and edited, regional magazines, as well as working for small publishers and independent authors. Information about her novels and her editing services can be found on her website: www.maryannwrites.com.

www.ingramcontent.com/pod-product-compliance
Lightning Source LLC
LaVergne TN
LVHW051544070426
835507LV00021B/2403